DEVELOPING PRIMARY SCHOOL THROUGH ACTION RESEARCH

Teachers' Reflections on Assessment at Key Stage 1.

Edited by
Pamela Lomax
and
Cynthia Jones

h

Hyde Publications

© 1993 Pamela Lomax and Cynthia Jones
and the authors of individual chapters.

All rights reserved. No part of this work
may be reproduced in any form or by any
means without permission in writing from
the publisher.

First edition 1993

Hyde Publications
57, Exeter Road,
Bournemouth,
Dorset. BH5 2AF

ISBN 1-874154-06-6

Typeset, Printed and Bound by
Bourne Press Limited, Bournemouth

Series Title: Accounting for ourselves.
Series Editors: Pamela Lomax, Jean McNiff and Jack Whitehead.

This series of books aims to provide a forum for practitioners to offer accounts of their own professional learning. The series aims to present quality accounts to show the systematic process of reflection, evaluation and modification of practice that is essential in promoting and sustaining improvement in educational contexts. Colleagues wishing to contribute to the series are invited to contact the Series Editors in care of Hyde Publications, 57 Exeter Road, Bournemouth, Dorset BH5 2AF. U.K.

Contents

1 **Introduction:**
Seven years on in an Assessment Community:
Implementing National Curriculum Key Stage 1 SATs
Pamela Lomax and Cynthia Jones 1

Part One: Reflections on Assessment 13

2 Reflections on Assessment and Testing in the Primary School.
Margaret Follows. 13

3 Teachers' Professional Judgements and the Management of Key
Stage 1 Assessment.
Brenda Spencer 21

4 Records of Achievement and Teacher Assessment: Reflections on
the Needs of Special Education.
Gail Larkin 27

Part Two: Implementing Standardised Assessment Tests ..31

5 Evaluating the Implementation of National Curriculum Key
Stage 1 Standardised Assessment Tests.
Margaret Follows 31

6 Implementing Standardised Assessment Tests: One Year On.
Margaret Follows, Patricia Ede, Alyson Rodway and Suzanne Waites. 47

7 Who's Testing Who's Testing What?
Barbara Abbey and Valerie Martin 57

Part Three: Developing the Whole School Context for
National Assessment 61

8 Observing Pupils and Listening to Parents: Aspects of a Primary
School Policy on Pupil Assessment.
Janet Mulholland 61

9 Developing and Implementing Records of Achievement to Meet
the Needs of Children with Special Educational Needs.
Gail Larkin 71

10 Formulating a Whole School Policy on Assessment for 3-8 Year Old
Children.
Brenda Spencer 81

Bibliography 93

INTRODUCTION:

1. Seven years on in an Assessment Community: Implementing National Curriculum Key Stage 1 SATs.

Pamela Lomax and Cynthia Jones

As teachers, we have lived in a decade of educational change in which many of our most cherished values about the way in which we believe children should be educated have come under attack. Although many in the teaching profession have always supported the principle of a core curriculum, few teachers could have guessed that the advent of the National Curriculum in 1989 would have been accompanied by the degree of central control over educational policies and structures that exists today. In fact few teachers who welcomed the notion of a National Curriculum could have foreseen its implications in terms of national assessment and testing.

The darker side of a national approach to schooling has been that many of the educational judgements that once were made by teachers are being made by bureaucrats and politicians. Pressures on teachers 'to put the orders of central authority into practice' appear to militate against their ability 'to exercise their professional judgement' (McBride, 1989, p.1). A fear being expressed by many educationalists is of the technocratisation of teaching, whereby teachers are expected to implement the educational judgements of others rather than make their own professional judgements, the result being a de-skilled profession (Carr, 1989, pp. 1-11).

In sharp contrast to the picture of educational gloom created by an increasingly centralised, bureaucratised and apparently technocratised education system has been the emergence of school focused and school based initiatives for teachers' professional development. McBride in his conclusion to a collection of edited accounts about the in-service training and education of teachers notes this development but seems pessimistic about its future.

> 'The greater control of INSET funds by schools has spawned the growth of school focused INSET... but only within a framework. Professional development is only a shadow on the wall of the real thing...... Teachers are expected to fit into various frameworks and institutions, to learn to teach the National Curriculum or to teach in areas considered national priorities by the central administration. I would prefer teachers and frameworks to grow together in an atmosphere of mutual respect' (McBride, 1989, p. 187).

We try to paint a more optimistic picture about the way in which teachers can work within the apparently strangling framework of national assessment to create something that is educationally worthwhile. In this book we present the accounts of teachers who demonstrate that they have been able to develop a process for managing change that is educational and collaborative, that enables the formation of critical communities and strengthens the authority of the professional educator in the formation and validation of educational work. The accounts take the form of extracts from longer case study programmes, and they provide evidence that teacher action research in the classroom and in the management of schools has enabled teachers to maintain their professional role within a context that is exerting pressure to de-professionalise them.

The accounts presented have two important elements in common. The first is that the teachers who have conducted them have participated in award linked in-service courses designed to support individual teachers researching their own practices and managing change in their own schools and classrooms: they have had the advantage of being part of the discipline and networking aspects associated with membership of a teacher action research group at Kingston University. Of more importance, the teachers themselves have been willing to work within the restrictions imposed on them and their school: they have succeeded in their innovative research because they have worked creatively within the spaces **they** made inside the constraints of their situations. Both these factors contribute to their success. Another factor is that although, in general, funding for teacher research and other forms of teacher professional development is very limited, the implementation of National Curriculum Key Stage 1 Assessment was a national priority and therefore schools received additional resources to support training.

Before looking at the action research approach that teachers used in their case studies, we would like to clarify the principles and events that led to the introduction of National Curriculum Key Stage 1 Assessment.

NATIONAL CURRICULUM KEY STAGE 1 ASSESSMENT

National Curriculum Key Stage 1 Assessment is a nation wide assessment of all children in State Primary Schools during the year in which the child reaches 7 years of age. It is an assessment of the child's attainment in relation to a number of core areas of learning set out in the National Curriculum.

The central platform of the assessment and evaluation of pupil performance at Key Stage 1 is contained within paragraphs 28 and 29 of the *National Curriculum 5-16 Consultation Document* (DES, 1987) which states:-

> 28: The attainment targets will provide standards against which pupils' progress and performance can be assessed. The main purpose is to show what a pupil has learned and mastered and to enable teachers and parents to ensure that he or she is making adequate progress. Where such progress is not made, then it is up to the school to make suitable arrangements for the pupil.

29. The Secretaries of State envisage that much of the assessment at ages 7 (or thereabouts), 11, 14 and at 16 in non examined subjects will be done by teachers as an integral part of normal classroom work. **But at the heart of the assessment process there will be a nationally prescribed task done by all pupils to supplement the individual teachers' assessments.** Teachers will administer and mark these, but their marking and their assessment overall will be externally moderated.

Here, then, began the pre-occupation with the Standard Assessment Test (SAT) that dominated the lives of many Year 2 teachers in the spring and summer of 1991, and which forms the basis for the work in this book.

The first statutory requirements appeared with the publication by the Department of Education and Science in July 1990 of *The Education (National Curriculum) (Assessment Arrangements for English, Mathematics and Science) Order 1990* (DES, 1990a). The main elements of the assessment arrangements appear in Paragraph 13.

'... the Order provides that the statutory assessment arrangements will have two elements:

a. an assessment by the teacher ('Teacher assessment') of each pupil's achievements in relation to the statutory attainment targets based on the pupil's ordinary classroom work over the course of the key stage and finalised in the Spring term preceding the end of the key stage.

b. one or more nationally determined Standard Assessment Tasks - or SATs - administered to each pupil and assessed by his or her teacher in the first half of the Summer term preceding the end of the key stage.'

The content of these paragraphs had been anticipated by the 1988 Report of the Task Group on Assessment and Testing (DES, 1988a), where the group had recommended that assessment of children's performance be made through the combining of teachers' own assessments and 'externally provided tests'. The Task Group on Assessment and Testing also sounded a warning note about this in their digest for schools where they said, 'If external tests are to provide the touchstone, they have to be carefully designed so that their results can be trusted'. They went on to point up the key role of teachers in encouraging children to exhibit a wide range of skills and abilities through effective modes of 'questioning' in whatever form was most appropriate for the child's capacities. 'The art of constructing good assessment tasks is to exploit all ... possibilities' (DES, 1988b).

Teacher Assessment (by its very nature) and the creative administration of the Standardised Assessment Tests (as recommended by the Task Group on Assessment and Testing) became the responsibility (in the main) of the classroom teachers associated with the year two cohorts, with moderators being provided through the offices of the Local Education Authority.

4   *Developing Primary Schools through Action Research*

The 1990 Order also directly involved the head teachers:

20: It will be for the head teacher of each primary school to determine the arrangements for administering SATs to individual pupils... Guidance on how to determine and record assessments based on an approved SAT will be contained in the instructions associated with each SAT. It will be for head teachers to ensure that schools follow these instructions.

and later in the same Order:

34: Head teachers and governing bodies are responsible for ensuring that their school is able to implement the assessment arrangements prescribed in the order. How they do so is a matter for each school. It is however a matter of good practice to develop the arrangements in the context of a comprehensive policy on assessment, recording and reporting linked to the school's wider curriculum policy'.

So the network of relationships between people, activities and policies which were to constitute the assessment of the National Curriculum at Key Stage 1 began to be put in place.

The School Examination and Assessment Council (1990a) in their *Guide to Teacher Assessment. Pack A.* represented these links diagrammatically.

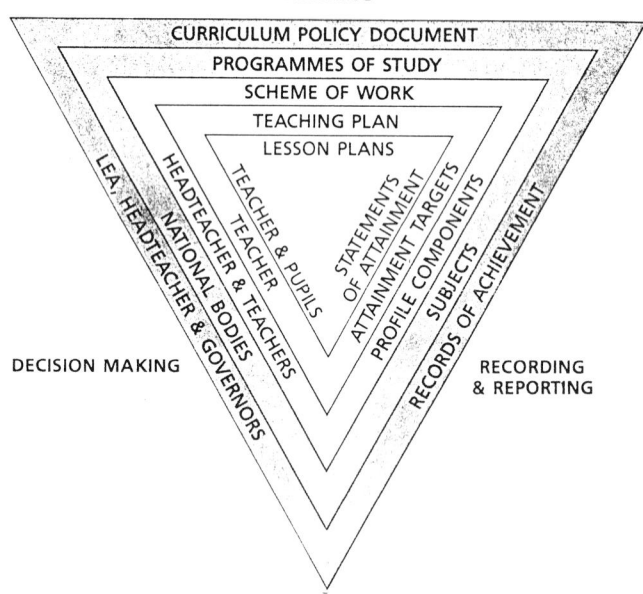

This representation allowed the theoretical links to be pointed up. The practical implications of this however were another matter, as were the tensions revealed by the lack of equivalence of the relationship between Teacher Assessment and the Standardised Assessment Tests in evaluating the performance of the child. In England and Wales, the results of the Standardised Assessment Tests are combined with Teacher Assessment, and if these two assessments match then there is no difficulty. However, if there is a discrepancy between the two types of assessment then the Standardised Assessment Test results take precedence and, as the BERA Task Group (1991) looking at assessment reported, 'this inflates the status of SATs at the expense of TA'. The situation where Teacher Assessment can take precedence over the Standardised Assessment Test results is clearly defined in the Order (DES, 1990a).

> 23 ...the Order provides that the assessment derived from the SAT evidence must be preferred, except where all the following conditions are met:
> a. the difference between the teacher assessment and the SAT assessment of a pupil's achievement in relation to the attainment target affects a pupil's overall profile component level;
> b. the teacher concerned, with the support of the head teacher, judges that giving preference to the SAT assessment yields a profile outcome which is not a true reflection of the pupil's attainments, and seeks a review on that basis; and
> c. the LEA which maintains the primary school agrees, in the light of the evidence presented by the school, that the alternative result should be accepted.

This cumbersome way of reconciling disagreement has been avoided in Scottish schools; here the results of Teacher Assessment and Standardised Assessment Tests are not combined but are seen as additional pieces of information.

The case study extracts in this book outline some of the ways in which senior teachers attempted to grapple with the complexities of the task ahead. At the time when the data for these case studies was being collected, little structural guidance had been given for how classroom teachers (and indeed whole staff groups) could be prepared for the task ahead. In many cases school policy for assessment and evaluation began to be overhauled at the same time as the Standardised Assessment Tests and Teacher Assessments were being implemented. For many schools, advice for additional training of staff and guidelines for the generation of a whole school policy document regarding assessment was not received by the schools until after the first wave of assessments had finished. Janet Mulholland (chapter 8) describes the general feeling of anger and inadequacy with regard to assessment felt by many teachers at this time.

> 'Effective planning had been precluded by not having received sight of the Standardised Assessment Tests as a complete package until a very late date, and several staff raised worries about teachers in general taking the blame for the effects of such blatantly rushed and overburdening assessment procedures having been imposed upon us.'

Thus teachers were not in a position where they could implement some of the suggestions made by the School Examination and Assessment Council in their guides to Teacher Assessment. Whilst all teachers would agree with the pronouncement in *A Guide to Teacher Assessment. Pack C.*, that 'assessment should not be allowed to slow down activity in the classroom' (SEAC, 1990c, p.53), they were also very much aware that the responsibility for such 'slowing down' did not usually rest with them. Other statements in the same pack reflect the need for systematic observation of children as a critical part of Teacher Assessment (see Janet Mulholland's account) and the integration of such activities into a whole school assessment policy, including matters associated with the reporting and publishing of results (see Brenda Spencer's account). This latter point also raises a significant difference between procedures recommended for England and Wales, and those implemented in Scotland. As the BERA Task Group (1991) report:-

> '...inter-school comparisons are explicitly encouraged in England and Wales, and further reinforced by the Citizen's Charter which proposes 'league tables'. In contrast, in Scotland, publication of results for the purpose of creating 'league tables' or other means of comparing schools is officially discouraged.'

The introduction of National Curriculum Assessment did put into high focus the need for a re-drawing or overhauling of the school assessment policy and procedures. The School Examination and Assessment Council's *A Guide to Teacher Assessment. Pack B* suggests that a school assessment policy should include agreed arrangements for the following 10 points:-

1. using the school's schemes of work to ensure progression and coverage of Programmes of Study.
2. monitoring the continuous use of assessment as part of the teaching and learning process.
3. teachers to ascertain whether they are consistent with one another in their interpretation of successful attainment of RoA.
4. recording achievement for RoA, for individuals and for the class as a whole; selecting, keeping and replacing samples of children's work.
5. recording children's achievements in other areas of the curriculum which are particularly valued by the school.
6. transferring individual and class records between teachers; deciding the extent and coverage of duplicated records to be held centrally; the transfer of records to another school when a child moves.
7. the form and frequency of reports to parents; access to records (by teachers, parents, governors, LEA); the form of summative school reports at the end of Key Stages.
8. a policy governing temporary disapplication and statementing of children; sharing the assessment process with the child.
9. inducting cover, support and newly arrived teachers into the whole school assessment policy.
10. reviewing all aspects of the school's assessment policy to ensure that it is integrated with and supports the whole curriculum.

Many teachers already shared these views prior to the publication of Pack B, and the accounts of Larkin, Mulholland and Spencer provide interesting examples of these.

Tensions and incompatibilities abound in the construction of any school policy document, but the early 1990's also saw a 'national' tension that touched on assessment policy in the form of the existing evaluative structure of Records of Achievement. Records of Achievement had been initiated into the secondary sector in 1983/4 by Sir Keith Joseph with the requirement that all secondary schools should have Records of Achievement structures in place for school leavers by 1990. The tension was created by the apparent contradiction between the requirement for records of achievement, with their emphasis on pupil achievement and ownership and the requirements of the criterion referenced National Curriculum assessment. This tension was partly reconciled by a statement made to the Task Group for Assessment and Testing by the Record of Achievement National Steering Committee which suggested:-

> 'Records of achievement, by giving weight to those aspects of the formal, informal or extra curriculum which lie beyond the foundation subjects, can present pupils' National Curriculum achievements within the context of the totality of their achievements and experiences in and outside the classroom. They can therefore redress any tendency on the part of those who make use of the National Curriculum assessments to ascribe undue importance to achievement against predetermined subjects attainment targets.'

Broadfoot (1988) makes a strong case for the characteristic features of Records of Achievement which stress pupils' self assessment, teacher-pupil review and target setting, being linked to National Curriculum testing, thus maintaining the principles upon which learner-centred assessment is based. Larkin's case study about the implementation of Records of Achievement into one primary school helps to highlight these elements.

The feedback received by the School Examination and Assessment Council from the first wave of national curriculum assessments has resulted in modifications being made to recommended national practice. The tests have become progressively more streamlined (and manageable) since their inception in 1990. However there are still many contentious areas of implementation (see the case study presented by Margaret Follows). In practical terms the 1992 Standardised Assessment Tests reduce attainment targets for maths, English and science; have more pencil and paper tests; include a new, optional, written comprehension test; introduce a finer grading of children's reading ability within level 2 in the reading aloud test; and drop some of the more time-consuming activities associated with the testing of children's science and mathematics application skills. Testing has also been allowed to be carried out over two half terms rather than one. New assessment arrangements have been put in place in relation to moderation and the role of the LEAs. Whether these are cosmetic or whether they have a real value in helping children's progress to be assessed and evaluated has yet to be seen.

THE ACCOUNTS

The accounts presented in this book are extracts from larger case studies, relating to the implementation of National Curriculum Key Stage 1 Assessment during 1990/1991, and are updated by two reports of the modifications made in 1991/1992. The accounts are written by head teachers and other teachers who used action research to ensure that the implementation of Key Stage 1 Assessment would occur in line with the educational values they held about good primary school practice.

The first part of the book contains three accounts in which contributors explore the meaning of assessment. In chapter 2 Follows explores questions such as, What is assessment? Why do assessment? Who is assessment for? and What do we assess? In chapter 3 Spencer examines some of the contradictions in the way in which assessment has been presented through the Education Reform Act, ministers' speeches about education and DES circulars. In chapter 4 Larkin considers the relationship between records of achievement and assessment. The conclusion reached in all three accounts is that, despite its close association with accountability, assessment should be an educational process, and policies on assessment should occur within an overall policy on teaching and learning that is appropriate for good primary school practice.

The second part of the book focuses specifically on the implementation and evaluation of Standardised Assessment Tests. Follows (chapter 5) monitored the implementation of National Curriculum Key Stage 1 Assessment as part of a larger action research project which was to do with developing the school as a co-operative, collaborative community. Highlighting the relationships between herself, her deputy, the two year 2 teachers responsible for assessing the children, and the LEA moderator, Follows carefully monitors the effect of LEA support and her own resource management on the implementation of assessment. Chapter 6 contains a transcript of a conversation between Follows and her colleagues about the changes made to Key Stage 1 Assessment in its second year of implementation. Chapter 7 is a more lighthearted review of the second year of testing, although it ends on a more serious note with the questions: What is different this year then? What is simpler? Who is it simpler for?

The final part of the book locates National Key Stage 1 Assessment within broader whole school issues. In chapter 8 Mulholland describes how she has developed a whole school policy and practice of assessment to provide an educative framework for testing. Her work has been concerned with developing a system for classroom observation of the whole child as a basis for making more specific assessments of targeted curriculum areas, and encouraging parental input into the assessments. Larkin's work in chapter 9 also stresses the importance of broadening rather than narrowing the knowledge base from which we make judgements of children's achievements. She argues for a record of achievement that contains information about the whole child, including achievement at home (thus involving parents) and at clubs. She favours a situation in which everyone who has anything to do with a child contributes information to the record. Her argument for using the record of achievement to include a record of what the child itself has targeted as important is built on by Spencer in the final chapter. She describes the success with which she developed a whole school assessment policy in which a key element was a policy on portfolios of children's work.

ACTION RESEARCH

All the cases studies described in this book and the extracts which are presented were supported by the action research perspective that has been developed at Kingston University. Although this perspective stresses that there is no one way of doing action research, it does recognise some essential ingredients for bringing about improvement in practice through action research. Lomax describes action research in the context of implementing educational change as:

> '... a way of working in which the teacher/researcher imposes a discipline on the monitoring and evaluation of practices that are expected to lead to educationally worthwhile outcomes. Essential elements of this process are a willingness (a) to highlight critically the values that illuminate one's own practice, (b) to make a disciplined study of that practice with a view to pinpointing the contradictions that exist between values and practice, and (c) to work towards a solution to the dilemmas that have been identified.' (Lomax, 1992).

The centrality of values to teacher action research is reflected in the insistence of the authors of Part One of the book that assessment is part of an educational process and therefore policy on assessment cannot stand distinct from policy on teaching and learning. Teaching and learning are not isolated activities. What goes on in schools and classrooms is the outcome of many different relationships, all of which demand co-operation and collaboration.

Constant review, by the action researcher, of the perspectives and feelings of others is essential for the successful management of change. The head teacher action researchers responsible for implementing Key Stage 1 Assessment whose accounts appear in this book were all mindful that 'others' needed to be involved as participants in the action, and not as informants or pawns. For example, in chapter 8, Mulholland argues that her enquiry was one which

> 'was concerned with teachers becoming innovators within the field of assessment'.

Follows (chapter 5) says,

> 'At the end of the teacher assessment period I came to realise that I had underestimated both the pressures placed on all teachers... and the difficulty key performers had in sharing their true feelings with each other. But I had underestimated .. teachers' capacity to adapt to change and to become members of a team working towards a common goal'.

The accounts also provide good examples of effective working within small support sets or with 'critical' friends who are colleagues drawn from within the research context who will help the researcher develop a self critical view of the research process (Lomax 1990, 1991).

Another key to successful action research is successful networking. The notion that we can create critical communities of teachers is reinforced in the title of this book. It reflects the particular way in which the teachers who have written the reports viewed the need to manage changes in their schools. It is not fortuitous that part 3 focuses on the need to locate Key Stage 1 Assessment in a whole school policy of assessment. The notion that change needs to be a whole school objective comes strongly through all the accounts. Follows (chapter 5) says:

> 'the primary aim was to develop a collaborative community of colleagues who would work together and support each other. The benefits ... from introduction of national testing in the school (came).... from the success with which the collaborative community became established and the collaborative response to the problems thrown up by National Curriculum Key Stage 1 Assessment.'

The research of all the teachers involved them in a rigorous form of enquiry that proceeded through a carefully monitored sequence of cycles that included planning, acting and evaluating. As action researchers they recognised the importance of acting to a plan but also being willing to change if necessary; of involving 'others' as fully as possible in evaluating the action which was carefully monitored; of becoming more ambitious in the scale of the improvements being sought and the sophistication of the data being collected as the research developed. During their research all teachers engaged in a process of on-going validation which involved periodically presenting evidence to substantiate claims about their work to colleagues for critique. Much of this evidence was taken from accounts written in their reflective diaries and was triangulated with data gathered in more traditional ways. All the accounts demonstrate these disciplines. The success of the research can be judged in terms of the way in which it led to increased knowledge rather than simply to successful action.

CONCLUSION

The accounts address some of the major issues related to the implementation of National Curriculum Key Stage 1 Assessment but they also address issues that relate more generally to assessment and its place within an overall policy for teaching and learning in schools. The current political climate is one in which the values underpinning much of our education are being attacked, at a time when the basis of teachers' professional authority is being dismantled for political and economic reasons. As we prepare this book we do not know what far reaching changes are planned for Teacher Education by a Government that seems bent on discontinuing college based initial teacher training. We do not know what repercussions this will have on inservice teacher education and cannot be certain that the type of work described in this book will survive future change. The uncertainty of Government policy on education is probably one of its most debilitating aspects and has affected teachers at all levels and in most institutions.

We have argued that within this scenario of political mismanagement there are teachers who are working creatively within the system to develop educationally worthwhile outcomes. We believe that it is this creative force of teacher action research that can maintain teacher autonomy and professionalism in the face of current de-skilling changes. We would like to end this introduction by quoting from a previous paper which outlines four of the strengths of action research which we think are demonstrated in the reports that have been presented. They are:

> '*Relevance*, to be able to conceptualise one's values in theories that are lived in practice; *emancipation*, to retain ownership of one's own values, theories and practices so that they are not appropriated by academic hegemonies; *democracy*, to value others' interpretations and recognise their right to participate in the definition of shared reality; and *collaboration*, to be able to work with and for others and for others to work with and for you'. (Lomax, 1986, p.49).

PART ONE: REFLECTIONS ON ASSESSMENT

2. Reflections on Assessment and Testing in the Primary School

Margaret Follows

The terms 'assessment' and 'testing' conjure up all sorts of images in people's minds. Often these memories are tinged with apprehension and a feeling of failure. Assessment for many of us has been an emotional experience and therefore many teachers prefer not to face young children with it too early in their lives.

There appear to be two contrasting interpretations of assessment:

> 'First ... an obsession with the measurement of performances (many of which are assumed to be relatively trivial) and an increasingly technical vocabulary... Secondly ... as the means by which schools and teachers sort out children for occupations of different status and remuneration in a hierarchical ordered society' (Satterley, 1989).

Satterley goes on to suggest that both these views of assessment are surprising when you trace the roots of the word 'assessment' which comes from the Latin 'assidere' - to sit beside, and the Latin 'educare' - to bring out. If we were to remain true to these roots, educational assessment would be seen as sitting beside the child and bringing out his/her potential by creating opportunities. But how do we reconcile this argument with the requirements of the age we presently live in, that is, the age of accountability, where testing and assessment are central procedures for establishing and monitoring that accountability process? Prior to the advent of the National Curriculum and testing, primary schools were judged to fall outside debates about accountability because:

> 'It is difficult to identify sufficient common ground or at least common language to begin to discuss the primary curriculum nationally, let alone carry out the kind of scrutiny and development required to establish a primary curricular framework and agreed objectives' (Bolton, 1985).

Are things different now? It would be a mistake to see the current emphasis on testing simply as a response to criticism of lack of accountability. Assessment should be seen as a central feature of any good teaching and learning process. Despite the views of Her Majesty's Inspector Bolton, primary schools have always (to some extent) employed their own methods of assessing children as part of teaching and learning. By careful consideration of assessment procedures teachers should be able to improve children's learning experiences as well as satisfying the demands of accountability. If this is achieved, teaching and assessment become inseparable, including all or some of the following: diagnosis, guidance, grading, selection, prediction and evaluation.

WHAT IS ASSESSMENT?

Assessment, evaluation, appraisal, testing and accountability are all part of the assessment picture and were included in the definition of assessment by the Department of Education and Science Task Group on Assessment and Testing. In their report, assessment was defined as:

> 'A general term embracing all methods customarily used to appraise the performance of individual pupils or a group. It may refer to a broad appraisal including many sources of evidence and many aspects of pupils' knowledge, understanding, skills and attitudes; or to a particular occasion or instrument. An assessment instrument may be any method or procedure, formal or informal, for producing information about pupils, e.g. a written test paper, an interview schedule, a measurement task using equipment, or a class quiz' (Department of Education and Science, 1988b).

Another way of clarifying the meaning of assessment is to distinguish between informal, formal and summary assessment. *Informal assessments* are continuously made in the course of daily teaching. They are often a matter of the moment, a check as to who is keeping up with the work, and a quick reinforcement with a smile or a nod. *Formal assessment* involves tests undertaken by children which are devised and set by the teacher or others who may never have seen or worked with the children. When these are set, the teacher and children know that the occasion is special in that the process of teaching is abandoned for the time being. The children must rely on their own resources and expect no help. Some of these procedures are likely to be 'standardized', either through the format set or because the results can be compared with results from a wider population of children of similar age or aptitude (these together may be regarded as formative assessments). *Summary assessment* is an attempt to draw together information and perceptions about children's progress over time. Summary assessment may be viewed as part of a record of achievement in the sense in which Gail Larkin describes records of achievement in chapters 4 and 9.

National Curriculum Assessment might appear to present yet another form of testing. Although it shares features of the three forms of assessment outlined above, it also has its own distinctive appearance; as Thomas argues, National Assessment tests:

> '..ought not to look like tests to the children and should, like teachers' informal assessments, be concerned with identifying what children can do ...In some ways they may look like mini schemes of work. They will be standardised in the sense that they should be presented and marked in prescribed ways' (Thomas, 1990).

WHY DO WE DO ASSESSMENTS?

Confusion about the nature of assessment is partially a result of the various purposes for which assessment is made. For example, assessment can be to do with:

> 'providing information for colleagues, recording work carried out by pupils, giving grades or marks, helping pupils review their learning, evaluating the effectiveness of teaching, helping teachers to plan, identifying pupils experiencing difficulties, maintaining standards, providing information for others outside the school...' (Ainscow, 1988).

Four main purposes of assessing children's work are: (a) to provide pupils with an indication of their individual achievements and progress; (b) to help the teacher identify areas of strength and weakness in pupils' learning and adjust subsequent teaching in the light of this; (c) to enable pupils to evaluate ways in which they can improve; and (d) to show others what standards of work have been achieved.

These purposes are reflected both in the materials coming from the Department of Education and Science and in the guidelines that have been produced by Local Education Authorities about assessment. For example:

> 'Assessment helps teachers to: decide what the next steps concerning your child's learning ought to be; make helpful comparisons with other children of similar age and abilities, and with the individual pupil's own capacity to succeed; identify difficulties' (London Borough of Croydon, 1986).

> 'It can further improve the effectiveness of the learning situation by presenting a positive feedback to pupils and providing information necessary to ensure continuity at all stages' (London Borough of Hillingdon, 1988).

From this quick review of the literature it seems that three main points have been identified for assessment. The first is so that the current teacher can decide what a child should do next. This is a highly skilled and complex activity and careful assessment helps teachers to make appropriate decisions more effectively. The second is so that the children can understand their own progress and be able to find ways of improving their own work. This purpose recognises the important role of the learner in his/her own assessment. The third is so that others can see the progress of individual children. This third purpose of informing others, parents in particular, raises complex questions about their reasons for wanting to know.

WHO IS ASSESSMENT FOR?

Assessment information is of interest to a number of different groups of people. The accountability aspect has already been discussed. In this respect assessment can provide information about the quality of education in the

Local Education Authority and identify schools with unsatisfactory achievements. The public will also be interested, particularly in relation to their role as parents. The Local Education Authority report *Improving Primary Schools (1985)* suggested that there were two motives behind parents' questions about their children's progress. Parents wanted to know whether their child was working well and making the progress of which he/she seemed capable. Parents also wanted to know how their child was getting on compared with others of about the same age. Teachers are the third group with an interest in assessment. The information is useful to them for a number of reasons: for example, in making decisions about the transfer of pupils from primary to secondary schools or in identifying individual children with special needs.

WHAT DO WE ASSESS?

Research from before the introduction of the National Curriculum and testing suggested that assessment in primary schools focused on the acquisition of knowledge, concepts and principles; the ability to apply the above to new situations; the ability to communicate; the ability to solve problems; and the development of attitudes (Duncan and Dunn, 1985). Assessment was seen to include both children's activities (written, pictorial, oral, aural activities, performance activities, self assessment, profiles) and teachers' activities (informal assessment, formal assessment, tests, observation, and so on). Black (1989) reporting on a study of primary school assessment in Scotland, reported a similar picture although the ability to solve problems was excluded from his list. His research suggested that teachers assessed children with a variety of methods including observation, oral work, written work and testing.

Much of the literature on assessment (Thomas, 1990; Ainscow, 1988; Gulbenkian, 1982) stresses the importance of seeing assessment as an essential element of teaching and learning and as an ongoing process that is integrated into the educational experience of each child. It is through careful selection of the most appropriate means of monitoring pupils' learning experiences that progress is maintained.

When teachers establish a routine for considering how assessment can become a regular feature of their planning, they are likely to contribute significantly to children's progress, and improve the quality of learning provided by the school as a whole. In this respect both what we assess and how we assess is to do with the learning experiences we provide. This was recognised before the implementation of the National Curriculum in the Gulbenkian Report (1982) which argued that schools need constantly to review the quality of their provision and their method of work, that is, engage in a continuing process of educational evaluation.

> 'The form and method of assessment should vary with the activity and the type of information sought. Assessments of pupils are not, nor can be, statements of absolute ability. They are statements of achievements within the framework of educational opportunities that have actually been provided. In some degree every assessment of a pupil is also an assessment of the teachers and the school (Gulbenkian, 1982).

From the point of view of the school as a whole there is a very clear interrelationship between teaching, learning, assessment, evaluation, school effectiveness and accountability. Thus: (a) assessment is a central feature of the teaching-learning process; (b) assessment is part of the continual evaluation of the effectiveness of the school; and (c) assessment is part of the accountability process.

By implication it means that planning for appropriate assessment requires consideration of national and local expectations as well as immediate school needs and the concerns of individual pupils. The importance of these issues has become more prominent with the introduction of the National Curriculum and its associated procedures for assessment and testing.

TESTING AND THE NATIONAL CURRICULUM

The political focus and a large professional preoccupation since the Educational Reform Act (ERA), 1988, has been the introduction of the National Curriculum and, more specifically, the requirement that children should be formally tested at ages 7, 11, 14 and 16. The National Curriculum provides a framework within which it is possible to carry out a National Assessment of children's achievements and through this a means of assessing teachers and making statements about the effectiveness of individual schools.

The Task Group on Assessment and Testing report endorsed many of the features of positive assessment discussed earlier in this chapter and a central feature of the report was that assessment should be seen as 'formative', that is, it should provide information to the teacher which influenced the organisation and structure for future learning both for the individual child and the classes as a whole. This was in contrast to a notion of 'summative assessment'. The report emphasised the importance of building on existing good practice.

> 'Promoting children's learning is the principal aim of the school. Assessment lies at the heart of this process. It can provide a framework in which educational objectives may be set and pupils' progress charted and expressed. It can yield a basis for planning the next educational steps in response to children's needs. By facilitating dialogue between teachers, it can enhance professional skills and help the school as a whole to strengthen learning across the curriculum and throughout its age range' (Department of Education and Science, 1988a).

By focusing on joint moderation and teacher dialogue, the report appears to support Joan Dean's view that 'one way of improving our understanding of children's learning and thereby our assessment of that process, is to engage in reflection with other teachers' (1983). This is also in line with the approach to the development of the assessment process advocated in this book, particularly in relation to an action research approach.

But does the implemented National Curriculum Assessment provide opportunities for making the experience of assessment a creative learning process? Is the moderation process a way of increasing potential for teachers' reflective practice? The main **functions** of moderation, according to the The Task Group on Assessment and Testing report, are hardly conducive to open reflection on practice. The Task Group on Assessment and Testing lists the two main functions as (a) to communicate general standards; and (b) to control deviation from the general standard by appropriate adjustments. However the **procedure** advocated by the Task Group on Assessment and Testing, that of 'group moderation', gave teachers the opportunity to discuss possible interpretations of pupils' learning experiences. It enabled teachers to clarify their judgements by having to explain them to others and in doing so reveal the basis of their assessments. The Task Group on Assessment and Testing recommended an emphasis on 'criterion-referenced' rather than 'norm-referenced' assessment, so that assessments were much more like the assessments teachers made about children every day. Also, it intended that each child's progress should be viewed primarily in relation to him/herself, and that he/she be provided with information on what the assessment was about. Since the Task Group on Assessment and Testing report, it has fallen to the School Examination and Assessment Council to advise on National Assessment practice. The School Examinations and Assessment Council has been largely responsible for the development of National Curriculum Key Stage 1 Assessment 1990 (pilot), National Curriculum Key Stage 1 Assessment 1991 (trial), and proposals for National Curriculum Key Stage 1 Assessment 1992.

IMPLEMENTING KEY STAGE 1 ASSESSMENT IN AN OUTER LONDON BOROUGH

The National Curriculum Key Stage 1 Assessment for 1991 had three elements: (1) Teacher assessment (2) Standardised Assessment Tests (3) Annual Reports to Parents.

Teacher Assessment

Teacher assessment was about continuous teacher assessment of pupils against published statements of attainment for English, Mathematics and Science. All Schools were expected to have similar teacher expertise and to have already established a continuous assessment process. It was assumed that appropriate assessment information, in the required format, was already available to support National Curriculum Key Stage 1 Assessment, so that a summary of the continuous formative assessment could be made at the end of the first Key Stage. The continuous assessment was summarised in February-March 1991 and judgements were made by each year 2 teacher about each individual pupil's level of attainment in each of 32 attainment targets in the 3 core subjects. Teachers had to decide which level (1,2 or 3) on each attainment target a child was to be allocated and to provide a reasonably precise indication about what the child knew, understood and was able to do. This information was summarised and the relevant document completed in March.

Standardised Assessment Tests

Standardised Assessment Tests were designed so that they looked like the pieces of work that each child normally undertook in the classroom. The intention was that they could be incorporated into the ongoing learning activities of the class. Each Standardised Assessment Test was written so that levels 1-3 of the attainment targets could be assessed. The teacher was required to consult the level each child had achieved in the teacher assessment in order to decide which activity each child would need to engage in. One of the intended purposes of the Standardised Assessment Test was to give the teacher the opportunity to confirm or revise the teacher assessment. In doing the Standardised Assessment Test each child was supposed to be able to demonstrate a range of competencies which the teacher would monitor by observing the process in which the child engaged as well as the result that was achieved (that is, a piece of writing or an oral account and so on). The Standardised Assessment Tests had to be administered to children in their final year of Key Stage 1 during April-May 1991. These children were 7 years old at some time during the year September 1990 to August 1991. This meant that some children were actually 6 years old when they took the tests. The children were assessed using the Standardised Assessment Test on 7 compulsory attainment targets, and 1 extra Maths and Science attainment target. Each Year 2 teacher was required to plan the administration of Standardised Assessment Tests within the classroom organisation, with particular consideration of how to group the children, how to sequence the assessment activities, and when and where to carry out individual reading assessments. Finally, the results of the Standardised Assessment Tests were entered on the appropriate documents, to satisfy requirements, both national and local. The statistical return was required by the Local Education Authority by the beginning of June 1991, and by the Department of Education and Science by the beginning of August 1991.

Reporting to Parents.

The first National Curriculum Key Stage 1 Assessment results were scheduled for report to parents in Summer 1992 although many schools chose to put parents in the picture much earlier. In my own school parents were told of the changes that had to be made to teaching and classroom organisation as a consequence of implementing the Standardised Assessment Tests very early on. The Standardised Assessment Tests results themselves were included in the written annual reports presented to parents in July 1991.

    A concern has been raised about the reporting procedures adopted and the extent to which they could lead to divisive comparison between schools. This is because information about individual pupils' achievement is not only available to parents but collected by the Local Education Authority for their monitoring of the school's delivery of the curriculum.

    If this information was to be made public, and taken out of context, it could lead to misinterpretation and possible damage to the public image of a school. The Task Group on Assessment and Testing suggested that care should be taken about the way in which the information was published and that generally it should be published 'only as part of a more general statement about the school produced by the school and authenticated by the Local Education

Authority. The Local Education Authority should provide material for inclusion in the statement describing the influence of factors, such as the socio-economic nature of the catchment area on a school's results' (Department of Education and Science, 1988a).

Nevertheless, teachers remain apprehensive about the possible outcomes of the national system of assessment and many of the fears that teachers expressed before the introduction of National Assessment have been reinforced in its first year of operation. Their concern stemmed from the fact that changes were being introduced too quickly; that questionable levels of resourcing were being made available to schools; and that there were serious delays in providing a clear definition of the assessment requirements or guidance for them. Teachers also has reservations about the form that assessment took: the single subject approach appeared to discount accepted theories about how young children learned; there was an implied linear progression which was not reflected in teachers' experience of how children actually learned; there were perceived problems in the proposed statements of attainment. Added to this there was little piloting of the curriculum and teacher assessment procedures before making them legally binding; there was a lack of in-service training support for schools inexperienced in close observation, record keeping and assessment. Finally, to make the management of the innovation even more daunting, its introductions coincided (for many schools) with the new financial arrangements being introduced under local management. Whilst the changes associated with the Task Group on Assessment and Testing reformulation of assessment procedures were clear, they nevertheless have not been without their critics.

CONCLUSION

In this chapter I have emphasised two important purposes for the teacher assessment of children's learning. They are:-

1. The improvement of the learning/teaching process itself - formative assessment.
2. The means of providing overall evidence of the achievement of children at the end of a set period of time - summative assessment.

While the first of these purposes has always underpinned school initiated pupil assessment, the second has received increasing emphasis as a result of the national statutory requirement to test the National Curriculum and publish the results.

Plowden (1967) argued that 'at the heart of the education process lies the child'. Richards (1984) suggested that 'the school curriculum is at the heart of education'. The Task Group on Assessment and Testing told us that 'assessment lies at the heart of the education process'. These quotations illustrate the radical changes and controversies that have occurred since the 1988 Education Reform Act with its increased emphasis on accountability and the evaluation of education in terms of its cost effectiveness and the extent to which pre-specified objectives are achieved.

3. Teachers' Professional Judgements and the Management of Key Stage 1 Assessment

Brenda Spencer

The Education Reform Act, 1988, was quite clear concerning the aims of the school curriculum. It said that curriculum should be balanced and broadly based and should (a) promote the spiritual, moral, cultural, mental and physical development of pupils at the school and of society; and (b) prepare such pupils for the opportunities, responsibilities and experiences of adult life. This curriculum coverage was then to be assessed.

> 'The main objective of the assessment arrangements will be to ensure that each pupil's attainment in a subject and elements within it can clearly be identified and the results used to help the pupil's progress. It is essential that the assessment arrangements establish what children know, understand and can do, in order that teachers and parents can identify their children's strengths and weaknesses, and plan the next stage of the education' (Department of Education and Science Circular 5/89).

This statement does not regard assessment merely as summative or as a device for teacher accountability. Rather, the requirement to assess a child's performance and understanding is seen within the context of planning for future progress, diagnosing areas of weakness and identifying strengths. John MacGregor M.P. and former Secretary of State for Education has tried to lay to rest the idea that assessment was a way of weeding out poor teachers. In a speech to teacher associations he declared:

> 'Assessment is intrinsic to the National Curriculum. It is nothing less than the means by which we can all keep track of what pupils have learned - as distinct from what they have been taught. As such, it is a key part of the teacher's professional equipment' (Department of Education and Science, 1990).

In his speech McGregor recognised that teachers have always carried out assessment but suggested that:

> 'What is new is the systematic framework for teaching and programming study afforded by the attainment targets. This demands ... a systematic approach to assessing achievement against those targets. It binds assessment to the curriculum. A National Curriculum without assessment would have been lop-sided and incomplete. It would have lacked the dynamism - the potential to lever up standards - that

assessment provides. If assessment is to fulfil this function it must both relate to what goes on in the classroom itself and be capable of integration with normal classroom practice. In other words, it must be manageable for teachers, because if it is unmanageable it will defeat its own purpose' (Department of Education and Science 1990).

This speech was revealing in a number of ways. Assessing achievement was seen to be desirable, not because of formative or diagnostic purposes but because of its potential to lever up standards. It was this aspect that was most blazoned by the popular press since it suggested that existing standards were inadequate. Missing from the actual orders about assessment was the concern MacGregor expressed for manageability and the delivery of assessment in the normal classroom situation. This was not achieved in 1991 even though some modification was made to the pilot assessment schemes of 1990.

The cornerstone status of assessment within the Education Reform Act was most clearly stated in the report of the Task Group on Assessment and Testing.

'Promoting children's learning is a principal aim of schools. Assessment lies at the heart of this process. It can provide a framework in which educational objectives may be set, and pupils' progress charted and expressed. It can yield a basis for planning the next curriculum steps in response to children's needs. By facilitating dialogue between teachers it can enhance professional skills and help the school as a whole to strengthen learning across the curriculum and throughout its age range' (Department of Education and Science, 1988a).

The Task Group report went on to state clearly that the assessment process should not determine what was to be taught and learned. Unfortunately, the balance between providing a framework in which educational objectives can be set but not determining what is taught is a difficult one to achieve. The Task Group on Assessment and Testing advised that assessment should be integral to the educational process, providing 'feedback' and 'feedforward' (assessment that was incorporated into teaching strategies). A further requirement sought by the Task Group on Assessment and Testing concerned moderation. Comparison should be facilitated across classes and schools, a common language and common standards should be available to parents, teachers and pupils. These were some of the promises featured in the early literature about Key Stage 1 Assessment.

FEATURES RELATING TO PRINCIPLES OF ASSESSMENT

Principles and purposes of assessment were carefully considered by the Task Group on Assessment and Testing. For the purpose of National Assessment it gave priority to four criteria:

(a) that assessment should be criterion referenced, i.e. related to various objectives;
(b) that assessment should provide a basis for future planning;
(c) that comparison of results should be facilitated across classes and schools. Moderation was seen as vital; and
(d) that assessments should relate to progression.

The four criteria underpinning National Curriculum Key Stage 1 Assessment that were to form the foundations of future national policy on assessment were that assessment should be:

formative: the appropriate way forward may be planned by looking at pupils' achievements;
diagnostic: learning difficulties can be classified and remedial help thereby devised;
summative: the overall achievement of a pupil should be recorded in a systematic way;
evaluative: the work of a school, or L.E.A. can be put under review.

The Task Group on Assessment and Testing concluded that the findings of assessment for different purposes would need to be aggregated. Purely summative assessment taken at the end of a phase of learning would throw no light on the educational history of a pupil and would not serve formative purposes. On-going teacher assessment would be a necessary adjunct to national formal testing in order to meet the full complement of assessment purposes.

MODE OF ASSESSMENT

A variety of tests were seen to be required to accommodate the full range of purposes of assessment. The many sources of information for assessment would be suited to different purposes. The Task Group on Assessment and Testing gave examples of some: general impressions; marking assessments; pupils' self-assessment; rating scales; checklists; practical tests; written tests. A wide variety of tasks were also envisaged. The written form was not the only mode. The Task Group on Assessment and Testing analyzed any one task in terms of three aspects or modes, which could be defined as follows:

the presentation mode: the method of delivery of the questions (oral, written, pictorial, video, computer, practical demonstration);
the operation mode: the expected method of working (mental only, written, practical, oral);
the response mode: pupils may answer in various ways (e.g. choosing one option in multiple-choice question, writing a short prescribed response, open-ended writing, oral, practical procedure observed, practical outcome or product, computer input).

In relation to good practice in constructing assessment tasks, the Task Group on Assessment and Testing suggests:

> 'The art of constructing good assessment tasks is to exploit a wide range (far wider than normally envisaged for tests) of modes of presentation, operation and response, and then numerous combinations, in order to widen the range of pupils' abilities that they reflect and so to enhance their educational validity.'

THE ADMINISTRATION OF ASSESSMENT

The teaching associations have been most concerned to discuss the issue of manageability of assessment. John MacGregor's awareness of manageability arose out of reports about the Key Stage 1 pilot assessment experiences. These were reported in the *School Examination and Assessment Council Recorder No. 6 Autumn 1990*, the newsletter of The School Examination and Assessment Council. The pilot assessments took place in three consortia of schools that had developed trial Standardised Assessment Tests in the core subjects. In all, the pilot involved some 18,000 pupils in over 600 schools from 54 Local Education Authorities throughout England and Wales. The report, based on the findings of Her Majesty's Inspector who had visited ten per cent of the pilot schools, remarked on the 'striking professionalism shown by teachers under very difficult circumstances' (p.8). Regarding manageability:

> 'The pilot made one thing very clear: there was simply too much to do, and there is no disagreement that in 1991 the Standardised Assessment Tests will need to contain less material and take much less time to conduct. The problems arose because of the number of Attainment Targets being assessed rather than the complexity of the material for assessing any individual attainment target'. (p.8)

As a result of the pilot scheme it was suggested that the Standardised Assessment Tests were modified so that they took no longer than about one half of the classroom time of a three week period. It was also emphasised that there was a need to allow flexibility in order that teachers could incorporate Standardised Assessment Test material within their own class topics.

The issue of manageability was still a cause of concern for teacher associations despite the modifications made by the School Examination and Assessment Council arising from the findings of the pilot study. A joint statement was issued by AMA, National Association of Head teachers, National Union of Teachers, PAT and SHA - surely a remarkable occurrence. Teachers were reminded that 1991 was a trial run. Statements from the Secretary of State said, '1991 is ... the trialling period for the national system as a whole...'. The professional associations advocated a reasonable work load. Assessment should not dominate the curriculum nor undermine the learning and teaching process. The statement emphasised:

'It is therefore important that head teachers and teachers should agree to use their professional judgement and where necessary moderate and adjust elements of assessment which are clearly not serving the best interests of a child or the class. Such actions would need to be justifiable on grounds of what is reasonable or unreasonable taking account of all the circumstances and possible alternatives' (AMA et al, 1991).

The National Association of Head teachers in *National Curriculum Helpline Guidance Note 11: National Curriculum Assessment* (p.1) offered three guiding principles in approaching the assessment task:

1. Avoid the excess of assessment;
2. Restrict the amount of administration and record-keeping that is required from teachers;
3. Be prepared to use professional judgement and to intervene to override elements of assessment which are clearly not serving the best interests of a child or a class.

The advice that was quite clearly being laid down for teachers was that they had a new responsibility for Key Stage 1 Assessment but they also were required to use their professional understanding as a resource. The National Curriculum could merely have reduced teachers to the role of functionaries. The development of a workable and wise system of assessment could call upon their professionalism in an unparalleled way.

ASSESSMENT PRACTICE AND SCHOOL POLICY

Principles and practicalities having been aired, these should all be incorporated within a coherent school policy. This overarching requirement was stated in *D.E.S. Circular 9/90*.

'Head teachers and governing bodies are responsible for ensuring that their school is able to implement the assessment arrangements prescribed in the order. How they do so is a matter for each school. It is, however, a matter of good practice to develop the arrangements in the context of a comprehensive policy on assessment, recording and reporting linked to the school's wider curriculum policy.'

The Surrey Inspectorate and the Surrey School Psychological service produced a document in summer 1988 *Towards an Assessment Policy in the Primary School*. Advice is given on drawing up a school policy for assessment. Schools are advised to identify first and agree the purpose of assessment within the school. The next stage is to decide what to assess. Whilst teachers are encouraged to identify attainment targets to which assessment is related, the direction is via analyzing concepts, knowledge, skills and attitudes children have acquired and utilise in their learning. How to assess is the next item on the agenda. Policy makers are advised (p.6):

'You will need to discuss a range of different methods of assessment and recording and choose those methods you feel are most appropriate for your school, will serve the purposes you have selected and which will be most likely to fit within classroom practice..... It will be helpful if the methods you choose are used in a similar way by all the staff. This will involve agreeing criteria for deciding when a child has understood a concept, knows some factual information, can perform a skill, or has developed a particular attitude' (p.6).

Policy makers then need to address how to record; what will be written and when; and the access of the record to interested parties. The final part of the document should address how the policy is used, monitored and reviewed.

SUMMARY

The review of the current literature relating to assessment produces an anomaly. Directives have emanated from the government via the Task Group on Assessment and Testing and the School Examination and Assessment Council relating to purposes and modes of assessment. The head teacher finds herself in the unusual position of not being able to juxtapose differing points of view concerning a variety of issues.

Educationalists are faced with legislation which places upon them the duty to carry assessment out and, whilst it must be admitted that this legislation is underpinned by exemplary principles, the agonies of manageability are still being felt throughout the system. Modifications of Standardised Assessment Tests are already being considered. Inevitably the balance of planning, teaching, learning and assessment has been thrown out of kilter by the summative Standardised Assessment Tests. The School Examination and Assessment Council and the government admit this.

The anomaly arises from the fact that teachers may have appeared as mere functionaries. However their professional judgement is being called upon as never before in Key Stage 1. This is encapsulated in the Task Group on Assessment and Testing's recommendation that 'teachers' rating of pupils' performance should be used as a fundamental element of the National Assessment system'. The review of the literature shows an unparalleled dependence on the quality of teachers' professionalism to make the fulcrum of the Education Reform Act ,1988–assessment–effective.

4. Records of Achievement and Teacher Assessment: Reflections on the Needs of Special Education

Gail Larkin

The introduction of the Education Reform Act (1988) has placed upon teachers a legal responsibility to assess children's learning both continually (from 5-16) and through standard assessment tasks undertaken at the end of significant stages in the child's education (the so-called Key Stages). This statutory requirement has served to highlight the crucial importance of teacher assessment in the evaluation and monitoring of pupil progress, an activity which has always been seen as central to the teaching role. My work with children in my mainstream first school, and a short-term secondment of one term to a special school served to focus my attention on the role of teacher assessment in records of achievement, and the implications of good practice for both records of achievement and also teacher assessment in relation to the Standardised Assessment Tests. In the rest of this chapter, I want to examine some of my reflections about the principles upon which we can construct a records of achievement policy within the new national testing requirements that will benefit all children, including those with special educational needs, both in special schools and in mainstream classrooms.

Throughout my career I have worked with many different forms of assessment and evaluation of pupil performance and have become very interested in the way that records of achievement sought to represent a more rounded picture of pupil performance. Introducing the pilot scheme in 1984, Sir Keith Joseph (the then Education Secretary) determined that by 1990 the structures would be in place which would allow all pupil school leavers to leave school with a record of achievement which reflected their academic successes, their prowess in cross-curricular skills and which described their personal and social qualities. The intention was that this document should be owned by the pupil, be negotiated with teachers and would serve as the basis for on-going documentation of further learning and skill acquisition. This mode of recording pupil progress with its focus on both formative and summative evaluations, and the partnership between teacher and pupil, reinforced my own beliefs about the role of a good record-keeping and assessment policy in school. These beliefs could be summarised as being that a good record keeping and assessment policy should:

1. ensure consistency in assessment procedures throughout the school;
2. reflect the curricular aims of the school;

3. ensure continuity and progression in learning;
4. emphasize positive achievements and personal qualities as well as academic abilities;
5. involve pupils in target setting and personal appraisal; and
6. give a basis for consultation with parents and outside agencies.

My experiences as a seconded deputy head teacher within a special school served to reinforce these beliefs about good practice. One of my concerns at the start of this secondment had been whether methods of record keeping and assessment for children with special educational needs was necessarily different from those in mainstream schools, or whether the principles of good practice in which I believed held good for both. If I was to believe the Task Group on Assessment and Testing Report (Department of Education and Science, 1988) statement that 'Assessment is at the heart of the process of promoting children's learning', the assessment of pupils for the promotion of effective learning should be a key tenet in all educational activities within both mainstream and special schools.

Particularly problematic was the specific role of teacher assessment in the total assessment process. Considerable debate had been and still is being engendered about the implementation and effectiveness of Standardised Assessment Tests, and the procedures associated with them are undergoing considerable change. However, the role of teacher assessment is central to both Standardised Assessment Tests and records of achievement and it is crucial to establish the dimensions of good teacher assessment and to consider how these can be developed. In theory, good teacher assessment is part and parcel of good early years teaching. In my experience, early years teachers (those who teach children aged 3-8) have as their primary focus the responsibilities of:

a) observing children's work and progress;
b) supporting children through appropriate action;
c) extending children's knowledge; and
d) assessing and recording children's work so that a full knowledge of each individual child's needs and achievements is reached.

My concern was that we needed to establish a clear link between this good primary practice and records of achievement, but the methods of record keeping currently used in many schools were too complicated and detailed to be either useful or relevant for the children concerned. Over-elaborate forms of assessment have the effect of daunting teachers, and generating a reluctance to complete the many elaborate pro-formae. The introduction of records of achievement could provide the impetus for a re-consideration of whole school assessment policy.

A useful working definition of records of achievement can be found in the School Examination and Assessment Council's report concerning primary school records of achievement (School Examination and Assessment Council, 1990). This states that the record of achievement '....is a file or folder including various assessments of the children's work, skills, abilities and personal qualities.... it gives details of achievement both inside and outside the classroom'. Such an assessment document could provide a flexibility and versatility that makes it appropriate for children in mainstream schools and also for children with special educational needs either in mainstream or special schools. It is particularly important for children with special educational needs that assessment should not confine itself to the academic dimension alone, but also reflect the all-round achievements of the child. Also critical (for all children) in the implementation of records of achievement is the central notion that it must concentrate on the positive achievements of the individual child, both socially and academically, which means that there is not an over-emphasis on the remediation of weaknesses. There is a positive movement forward for the child who is working from a basis of what can already be done and what can be built on, rather than the developing of a pre-occupation with what has not been done or achieved. The School Education and Assessment Council believes that adopting the approaches used in a record of achievement will enable:-

> '... children and teachers to discuss progress together, and children are often involved in assessing their own progress and in setting their own targets for continued learning....... it will ensure planned continuity and learning development and produce a cumulative record of an individual child's all-round achievements. It records positive achievement and ideally involves children, parents and teachers in the process.... Close assessment against tight objectives and appropriate target setting are important for all children, particularly those with special educational needs.'

An obvious implication of this is that the compilation of the record must involve the co-operation of different people. Active participation by all staff members concerned with a particular child is essential, as the success of any such an assessment scheme depends on the techniques and procedures used in the classroom. Records of achievement with their great emphasis on teacher/pupil evaluation and negotiation should be owned by the parties concerned and therefore require their full involvement.

The special function that records of achievement serve in special schools was reinforced by Her Majesty's Inspectors in their 1989 survey (HMI, 1989). It was argued that the emphasis on the therapeutic role of the school needs to be balanced by greater consideration of the educational needs of the pupils, and, by implication, with the assessment of these needs. I believe that the idea of a record of achievement is particularly suitable for children in special schools where the more orthodox assessment via Standardised Assessment Tests is not appropriate. Using the type of approach demanded by the records of achievement gives the most severely disadvantaged child the opportunity for his or her experiences and achievements to be noted and recorded. Indeed in some special school contexts the child's advocate enters into the negotiating of assessment with the teacher concerned.

The importance of developing records of achievement in special schools goes alongside the view held by many Local Education Authorities that the National Curriculum should be provided for children with special educational needs. This means that the special school curriculum should provide a broad, balanced and differentiated programme for a wide range of learning needs. The London Borough within which I work, for example, in its statement of policy makes clear its expectations that '....all pupils with special educational needs, whether statemented or not, should have access to the same broad, balanced and relevant curriculum as their peers' (London Borough of Merton, 1991). The Borough's view that 'Continuity and progression are important because they ensure that a pupil passes through the phases of school life with a clear sight of the next step' reinforced my view that a good record keeping system was of paramount importance in ensuring progression and continuity for all children and particularly those with special educational needs.

The outcome of my reflections concerning assessment in both the special school and mainstream contexts confirmed me in the view that the formal requirements of Standardised Assessment Tests and the on-going more informal assessments that provided the thrust for pupil progress could come together in an appropriate record of achievement. The positive benefits for pupils (with the opportunities to develop self-evaluation skills and to feel more fully part of the assessment procedure) and for teachers (with the development of a structure which allowed on-going assessments to be integrated with statutory assessment requirements) provided further impetus for my reflections. The outcome was the action research study reported in chapter nine.

PART TWO: IMPLEMENTING STANDARDISED ASSESSMENT TESTS

5. Evaluating the Implementation of Nation Curriculum Key Stage 1 Standardised Assessment Tests

Margaret Follows

I was appointed head teacher to an outer London borough infant school in September 1989. Prior to this the school had been through an unsettled period due to threatened amalgamation and staffing problems. My first year saw a major building programme, a new nursery class and a number of new appointments, including the deputy head teacher. This happened alongside the implementation of the new requirements of the 1988 Education Reform Act with a delegated budget from April 1991, and the need to implement National Curriculum Key Stage 1 Assessment in the spring and summer of that year. At the same time we were to continue the Local Education Authority programme for testing all seven year old children in reading (Neale test) and mathematics (Thameside test).

During 1991 there were 230 children on the school roll placed in eight classes. This included two part time nursery classes, three reception classes, two year 1 classes and two year 2 classes. There was an additional 1.7 teacher support and a nursery nurse. The year 2 classes which were to participate in National Curriculum Key Stage 1 Assessment had 24/25 children in each. They included 6 children at various stages of statementing and 7 children with English as a second language. The school was also an Local Education Authority pilot school for the evaluation of National Curriculum Key Stage 1 Assessment.

THE RESEARCH

The research was part of a larger action research project which aimed to develop the school into a co-operative, collaborative community of teachers (Follows, 1992). The implementation of National Curriculum Key Stage 1 within this broader aim was a particularly challenging venture because it was a change enforced from outside the school. By monitoring the way in which I facilitated the development of co-operation within the school at this period, I was able to evaluate National Curriculum Key Stage 1 Assessment also.

CYCLES OF ACTION RESEARCH

The project can be divided into three cycles of action research. The first cycle from January-March 1991 focused on the teacher assessment aspect, but also established the basis for work during the Standardised Assessment Tests period. The second cycle from April-May 1991 focused on the administration of Standardised Assessment Tests. The third cycle (June-July) was to do with reporting to parents and evaluating the project as a whole.

The main features of the project were: (a) establishing initial working partnerships between teachers and moving these towards the development of whole school partnership; (b) allocating resources to support the work; (c) implementing training initially for key teacher performers and later for all staff; (d) reporting to the Governors and establishing their support; (e) attending Local Education Authority training days and cluster group meetings and working with the Local Education Authority Moderator; (f) involving the whole staff in evaluating the work.

The key performers consisted of the head teacher (myself), the deputy head teacher to whom I had delegated responsibility for implementing National Curriculum Key Stage 1 Assessment, and the two teachers responsible for the year 2 classes that were to be assessed. The Local Education Authority advisory teacher who was to moderate National Curriculum Key Stage 1 Assessment was also to become a second critical friend as the work progressed. I saw myself and the deputy head as facilitators who would play a supportive role. I met the deputy head each week throughout the project in a conscious attempt to develop our partnership role. I considered it important that these meetings should take place in prime school time and should take precedence over all but the most urgent interruption. Our initial task involved building the self confidence of the year 2 teachers so that they could take responsibility for the task of assessment themselves. In order to do this we met them daily. Once this had been achieved I hoped to establish whole staff confidence in this way of working in order to involve all the staff in changing whole school policy/practice on teacher assessment.

During the action research I kept a reflective diary. My concerns at the start of the project were very clear. They were about: (a) how the two teachers in year 2 could manage the assessment tasks; (b) how the children in year 2 could undergo assessment without too much disruption to their normal routine; (c) how fruitful collaboration could be established between the staff to be involved as key performers in the assessment work; (d) how the rest of the staff could be involved in planning for changes to existing whole school assessment arrangements; (e) how an outsider, that is, the Local Education Authority Moderator could be involved.

THE ACTION

A key factor in the early success of our strategies was the provision of non contact time for year 2 teachers so that they could be released simultaneously to engage in joint planning. Later I was able to provide classroom support during the administration of Standardised Assessment Tests and non contact time for year group teams to meet and finalise the written reports to parents. Other staff resources included my own release with the other key performers to attend Local Education Authority training days and meetings between members of cluster group schools, and the use of school training days for whole staff discussion of assessment issues. Tables 1-3 (reproduced at the end of this chapter) are a summary of some of the key events that occurred in the three cycles of action research between January and July 1991.

Staff meetings

I used staff meetings as arenas in which I attempted to engage all staff in what I was trying to develop as a collaborative community. One of my first strategies was to involve all colleagues in planning staff meetings for the term ahead. The key performers in the research were expected to report back to staff meetings to keep colleagues informed about the progress of National Curriculum Key Stage 1 Assessment. In fact all the decisions that were made about National Assessment were agreed at meetings of the whole staff before being put into operation.

Staff training days

Staff training days served a different function from staff meetings. At the beginning of January we had a staff training day in which we discussed ideas for a teaching/learning policy. Although staff had not tuned in to the implications of Key Stage 1 Assessment at that time, I was clear that we would have to augment a policy for teaching/learning and relate it to assessment if assessment was to be productive in the education of the children. The two whole school In-Service Education and Training days which followed the Local Education Authority training days were concerned with engaging the whole staff in discussion about assessment arrangements. At the staff training session following the first Local Education Authority training day (25.2.91) there was minimal awareness by the staff that assessment was to be a whole school issue. By the second of these days (18.3.91) the year 2 teachers were able to outline new ideas for change. Changes to existing assessment procedures and joint planning for the introduction of new ongoing forms of assessment were agreed by all the staff. This involvement of the whole staff continued to accelerate throughout the period with all staff being involved in finalising plans for the Standardised Assessment Tests period (16.4.91), planning an agreed format for reports to parents (17.4.91) and evaluating the Standardised Assessment Tests period (22.5.91).

Local Education Authority Training Days

Two training days were provided by the Local Education Authority and these were attended by myself, the deputy and the two year 2 teachers. These were important in several ways: we gained confidence from knowing that we were up to date with requirements for assessment; we were able to share uncertainties with teachers from other schools; and of major importance - these training days enabled the start of immediate collaboration between the deputy and the year 2 teachers. On the first of the Local Education Authority training days (11.2.91) we were able to plan the teacher assessment period. Teacher assessment was to run from February-March 1991 when the teachers of year 2 children had to make assessments of all children in 3 core curriculum areas (mathematics, English and science). Preparation for the teacher assessment period involved discussion of appropriate support for the year 2 teachers and completing the teacher assessment proformae. By the end of the second Local Education Authority training day (6.3.91) we had made plans for the Standardised Assessment Tests period and the year 2 teachers had gained sufficient confidence to complete the Standardised Assessment Tests proformae themselves.

Meetings of personnel from cluster group schools

There were four meetings between members of the cluster group schools. These were organised by the Local Education Authority Moderator for year 2 teachers from different schools to share 'concerns' during the teacher assessment and Standardised Assessment Tests periods. These meetings were attended by the year 2 teachers.

Support from the Local Education Authority Moderator

The Local Education Authority Moderator played a vital role in the teacher assessment period. Her main role was to moderate children's work by comparing different examples. She also visited the school to moderate Standardised Assessment Tests, which meant observing teachers and children when involved in Standardised Assessment Test activities and reaching a consensus about the levels achieved by children. She visited the school on several occasions to liaise with the key performers about the moderation of the children's work. She was involved in the planning of the teacher assessment period and its evaluation on 19th April. She also attended the staff training days on 25th February and 18th March and spoke to the whole staff about aspects of the assessment.

National Association of Head Teachers

During 1991 the local executive of the National Association of Head Teachers were monitoring National Curriculum Key Stage 1 Assessment in local schools and I was involved in a number of meetings where head teachers discussed feedback from this monitoring exercise.

Meetings with support set and critical friend

During the research I was supported by a group of teachers associated with Kingston University who were also engaged in the management of change. My first critical friend was a head teacher from a special school with whom I had worked closely before. The Local Education Authority Moderator became my second critical friend. The support set and critical friend provided me with safe contexts in which I could discuss the research. They also provided me with arenas within which I and some of my colleagues from school could test out the claims we were making about implementing change. Two such validation meetings occurred during 1991 and I was further able to validate the work by presenting a paper at the Annual Conference of the British Educational Research Association in August 1991.

INTERIM REFLECTIONS

At the end of the teacher assessment period I was able to take stock. I was conscious that I was a relatively new head teacher, that I was committed to an ethos of collaboration which my colleagues might not share, that the school had suffered from past inconsistent management, and that it was a time of incredible uncertainty with mixed messages about National Curriculum Key Stage 1 Assessment coming from the Department of Education and Science, the Local Education Authority and the media. At the beginning I had been resistant to the changes I was being expected to implement and angry that resources had to be taken from other areas of school activity to support National Curriculum Key Stage 1 assessment. I had also been uncertain about my plans for tackling the situation. Some of these early doubts were clearly recorded in my research diary:-

(1) How did I feel about the deputy and the year 2 teachers gaining more expertise than myself with National Curriculum Key Stage 1 Assessment?

(2) Would the National Curriculum Key Stage 1 Assessment period counteract my aim to develop a collaborative community?

(3) If I succeeded in establishing collaboration between the year 2 teachers could I extend this to other year groups and the whole staff?

(4) What were the true feelings of the staff directly involved with the project about: (a) changes to their classroom organisation and curriculum planning; (b) shared responsibility and being a member of a co-operative group; (c) the need for improved management of the curriculum; (d) the need for changes to the assessment of children's work throughout the school; (e) their ability to maintain/improve the education of the children?

At the end of the teacher assessment period I came to realise that I had underestimated both the pressures placed on all teachers (not just the key performers) and the difficulties that key performers had in sharing their true feelings with each other. But I had underestimated also teachers' capacity to adapt to change and to become members of a team working towards a common goal.

STANDARDISED ASSESSMENT TESTS

The Standardised Assessment Tests were administered between April and May 1991 by the year 2 teachers to small groups of children while a support teacher had responsibility for the remainder of the class. The tests took place in the normal classroom where teachers were able to plan for flexible groups of children and use a variety of locations depending on the activity. The tests consisted of a compulsory group of seven target attainments and a choice of one from four maths targets and one from three science targets. The final targets were:

Compulsory group
Reading [EN2]. Writing [EN3]. Spelling [EN4]. Handwriting [EN5]. Using/applying mathematics [MA11]. Number [MA3]. Exploration of science [SC11].

Choice group
Shape/space [MA101]. Uses of materials [SC6].

EVALUATING NATIONAL TESTING

An advantage of being part of the sample of Local Education Authority schools where national testing for Key Stage 1 was being monitored was that I was able to compare the Local Education Authority evaluation results with the data generated in the school [Croydon Local Education Authority, 1991].

The Local Education Authority report suggested that in some instances the Standardised Assessment Tests had identified areas in which teachers had underestimated children in their assessment of them although in the majority of instances the Standardised Assessment Tests confirmed teacher assessment. Our experience was that for eight of the nine targets there was agreement between the test result and teacher assessment.

Within the Local Education Authority most classes took the whole of the 6 week period allowed and children enjoyed a 1:4 teacher pupil ratio and in most instances did not feel stressed by the activities. This was in line with our own experience.

> 'I don't think the children were stressed by the actual Standardised Assessment Tests; they just thought they were doing special work and because of the support, we could give them our undivided attention' (Year 2 teacher).

Our experience suggested that all the tests were appropriately child centred and all the tests were enjoyed by the children. It was felt that this was due both to the way in which the test activities had been presented but also to the way in which the teachers had been able (without interruption) to work with the children (due to classroom support). Both year 2 teachers commented on the appropriateness of the practical nature of the activities, particularly given the limited previous experience of their particular children. However, as I argue elsewhere in this chapter, the 1:4 pupil teacher ratio was achieved at great cost to the school. The resulting quality experience for the children during the test situation should not be seen as the simple result of the introduction of national testing. In fact, our experience of the testing raised some serious questions about the tests themselves.

Were the levels of achievement appropriate for each Standardised Assessment Test?

Teachers were concerned about levels for a number of reasons: (1) for some tests the range of acceptable responses was too narrow eg. EN2: reading; (2) for some tests it was possible to pass at level 3 and fail at level 2, e.g. MA 10: shape/space; (3) some of the levels represented difference rather than progression (EN2: reading level 1/2).

Was the time taken to complete the tests appropriate?

Teachers thought that 5 of the 9 tests took too long to complete.

Were the tests valid?

The teachers were concerned that some tests were: (a) inappropriate for the maturation level of 7 year old children: for example, MA 1/2: required computation/instant recall; for example, MA 10: required complex verbalisation of actions too difficult for those with limited language skills; (b) too narrow to give a full picture of the child's achievements, for example, EN2 Reading: this concentrated on testing memory rather than other reading skills; EN 1/2/3 Writing: this was to do with writing a story rather than factual writing; (c) not testing what they purported to test, for example, EN2 Reading: the choice of books was too wide, particularly at level 2, so that success was partly due to choice of book rather than ability to read; (d) containing ambiguities leading to problems in assessing accurately, for example, SC 1/6: very similar to some of the Maths; MA 1/3/10: interpretations varied for teacher guidance/intervention/ guidance. On the one hand it was possible for the teacher to ask leading questions that did not require the child to reason through the problem, and on the other to give too little direction.

Were the tests fair?

The tests were deemed unfair (a) in relation to moderation; for example, some of the activities were ambiguous to the extent that the teacher was not always able to identify a correct answer; and (b) in relation to the organisation of the testing, thus: (1) it was difficult for teachers to provide an 'equal new experience' for all children as the tests were carried out in the classroom and the first group could be observed by children to be tested later; (2) it is likely that teacher administration of the test improved with practice.

Were the tests too complex?

4 tests were considered too complex to provide an accurate assessment of a child's achievement. Particular reference was made to the complexity of the

paperwork for EN 1. On the whole it was felt that teachers were able to adapt the assessments to a normal classroom situation. Some Standardised Assessment Tests activities were thought to be suitable as a basis for teacher observation which could be adapted to normal classroom organisation.

CLASSROOM EXPERIENCE

Another positive result of the testing identified in the Local Education Authority report was that in some cases children had learned for the first time to work as a group and teachers had reflected on ways in which they grouped and questioned children. Certainly our own experience supported this and I would stress the importance of collaboration in building the confidence of the year 2 teachers, one of whom, it should be remembered, was in her first year of teaching. There was also evidence that the deputy, who was responsible overall for National Curriculum Key Stage 1 Assessment, also benefited professionally from the collaboration.

THE CURRICULUM

The Local Education Authority report was less complacent about the influence of national testing on the curriculum. Most schools and year 2 classes had experienced changes of routine during the term. Most felt the curriculum had narrowed and that Music, Physical Education and Art had suffered. Children were not being heard to read on a regular basis by the class teacher. Issues of the narrowing of the curriculum and hearing children read during the test period were seen to be in need of addressing as whole school planning issues.

Our experience reflected some of these Local Education Authority concerns. Both year 2 teachers expressed concern at the disruption to children's learning which would have been even greater without teacher support in the classroom. They both felt that their delivery of the curriculum had been adversely affected by having to administer the tests. What they considered to be quality teaching time had been increasingly disrupted. This related both to continuity and breadth of curriculum delivery. There was limited use of the computer, the design technology work stations, creative activities and practical activities. There were fewer changes to the displays of children's work on the classroom walls and a more limited use of the book lending scheme. Greatest concern was expressed about the limited and irregular time for hearing children read.

> 'This term, continuity went completely from my point of view... I was jumping from one thing to another, a bit of Standardised Assessment Test here, a bit of ordinary work there ... with really no sort of integration. We worked out our theme for the half term, but I don't think it had any relevance to what we were doing ...my children have suffered so much

because I haven't heard them read..it wasn't covered at all. We've cut out television. Art and Physical Education have suffered too. I don't think the children made any progress this half term' (Year 2 teacher A).

'I wasn't teaching really. I was jumping through hoops to suit the paperwork . . . after 3 weeks you knew your children were missing out. You knew your class was a mess' (Year 2 teacher B).

EFFECT ON PUPILS

The Local Education Authority evaluation reported that some teachers noted retrogressive behaviour and work patterns among the children. Most teachers thought that children's learning had only been maintained and was not as 'far ahead' as usual for this time of year. Least stress was noted in classes where work had been planned around a topic and where children had experienced independent learning and focused group teaching before the test term.

Our own experience was a little different due to historical circumstances in the school which had favoured a more formal approach in the past which I was currently working to change. This meant that at the same time as the teachers were administering the tests, I was encouraging them to change their classroom practice towards a more collaborative, child centred approach. The teachers had little past experience of having a second teacher in the classroom which happened during the administration of Standardised Assessment Tests. These factors probably resulted in both teachers being a little over cautious in their expectation of children's ability during the testing.

EFFECTIVE SUPPORT

All year 2 teachers in the Local Education Authority sample had received additional adult help. This raises questions about the nature of the support that schools were able to provide. In my own case, because I considered it a whole school staff training issue, I was willing to combine the delegated In-Service Education and Training budget and the supply budget to buy in additional classroom support without depleting support in the rest of the school. I provided additional classroom support over and above that already provided to release teachers for planning. This amounted to an additional teacher for 1 day per week during a 6 week period.

The Local Education Authority evaluation suggested that consistency was a key element in effective support. It was best where the adult was known to the children and in place in the classroom before the test term. Support was particularly effective if time had been given for collaborative planning between support teachers and year 2 teachers. I was fortunate in being able to enlist the help of part time teachers who were already known to the children, thus minimising potential disruption. Despite this it was impossible to maintain familiar routines and there were indications that some children suffered. One year 2 teacher noted:

> 'The children felt insecure as the routine changed and there were different people in and out of the classroom. Children who were immature at the beginning of the year reverted to clinging to me in the mornings' (year 2 teacher).

ADMINISTRATIVE LOAD

All teachers in the Local Education Authority sample noted a change in the nature of their non contact work with time being spent on administration duties other than planning for focused groups, displaying work and undertaking curriculum leadership responsibilities. Some teachers thought that planning was easier because planning for Standardised Assessment Tests had been done already but others stressed that planning for the term was necessary for the whole class and not just for the test groups.

Our own experience supports part of the Local Education Authority picture. Although the classroom support eased the additional burden of having to administer the tests, the year 2 teachers were faced with an overall increase in preparation in order to maintain the overall curriculum planning for all children. Extra meetings had to be arranged to include support staff in this planning. The year 2 teachers spent extra planning time considering both the resourcing and approach needed for administering the test activities and collecting information after the completion of the tests. The extra work resulted in a detrimental effect on both year 2 teachers' health, and both had absences from school as a result.

My policy from the start was to delegate responsibility for National Curriculum Key Stage 1 Assessment to the class teachers concerned. The evaluation carried out in the school suggested this was a successful strategy. The year 2 teachers recognised the development of their own self confidence and expertise because of delegation.

> 'Delegation ... you gave us the supply ... we did the job' (Year 2 teacher A).

> 'Non involvement was a blessing. It was difficult enough liaising with supply and part timers, finding room to work, and so on. We worked it out as we went along. If we had had to consult it would have been so time consuming' (Year 2 teacher A).

> 'I felt that the initial sessions at the Teachers' Centre with the head and deputy were very useful. Decisions were made early on. The day planner was good, then minor details were left to us to sort out. Again discussion had to be taken pragmatically. Sometimes the deputy and head were not available because of other commitments. I felt this was a good thing. You had to make your own decisions' (Year 2 teacher A).

CONCLUSION

In conclusion I would like to comment on the degree to which we, as a staff, have become a critical community of practitioners during the stressful time of implementing National Curriculum Key Stage 1 Assessment.

The costs to schools of implementing National Curriculum Key Stage 1 Assessment should not be underestimated. For many schools the energy that has been put into National Assessment has come from that which should have gone into their continuing development as organisations. In my own school the support given to year 2 teachers has been at the expense of support that might have gone to curriculum co-ordinators, to the probationary teacher or to other year groups. A review of the activity indicates that there has been disruption to established routines, and children's stability has been affected. The time taken to test reading has been at the expense of hearing children read. The brunt of the disruption has been put on the children and teachers in year 2 classes. The time in which these teachers have planned a balanced curriculum has been put over to the administration of tests, their teaching contact with children has been reduced, the curriculum in their classrooms has been narrowed, their children's work has remained undisplayed, and they have spent less time with children who have special needs. They have also paid a personal price as assessment has encroached on their private lives and has effected their normal good health. These difficulties have been exacerbated by the lack of sensitivity with which the changes have been brought about and by the hostile media coverage. There have been high levels of tension amongst staff and a general feeling of uncertainty that at times has reduced morale.

However, in the school that was the focus of this action research study, the primary aim was to develop a collaborative community of colleagues who would work together and support each other. The benefits that came from the introduction of national testing in the school can be seen as coming directly from the success with which the collaborative community became established and the collaborative response to the problems thrown up by National Curriculum Key Stage 1 Assessment. All the key performers in the school have agreed about the value of joint discussion and collaboration during the period of implementing National Curriculum Key Stage 1 Assessment. There have been some reservations. The deputy was concerned that the degree of involvement achieved by the key performers sometimes conflicted with other school responsibilities. Nevertheless she recognised the benefit of collaboration to her own and others' professional development. This perception was also shared by the year 2 teachers.

> 'It was very useful for me personally ...it helped develop my relationship with year 2 teachers and gain their trust ... it also made the year 2 teachers feel their role was valued. All possible opportunities were used (but) obviously these were limited to some degrees by circumstances.' (Deputy head)

> 'The role of the deputy head teacher or assessment co-ordinator gave me, especially as a probationer, the knowledge that the back up of a final decision maker was there if necessary.' (Year 2 teacher B)

Both year 2 teachers recognised the advantages of their collaboration with each other, believing that it would have been more difficult to work in isolation because of problems related to insufficient support, lack of self confidence and the requirements to standardise the administration of both teacher assessment and the tests.

'Most time would have been taken cogitating. Consultation and joint discussion makes for more confidence and sanity ... when discussing and standardising ... which would have been impossible alone.' (Year 2 teacher B)

'Problems were solved as they arose. We helped each other to find the most economic way of fulfilling tasks and of sorting out the paperwork.' (Year 2 teacher A)

'I found working with year 2 teacher B really easy ... we negotiated ourselves out of difficult situations knowing we could rely on each other to fault find without guilt.' (Year 2 teacher A).

It was also very noticeable that year 2 teachers' attitudes towards teacher assessment and testing had changed from a passive disinterest to an appreciation that it had brought about small group teaching/learning situations and cooperative teaching situations that were seen to be of value. It was also noticeable that the role of support staff in their classes had begun to be more integrated into the classroom organisation.

'The administering of Standardised Assessment Tests has facilitated the professional development of year 2 teachers and other teachers too. Both year 2 teachers have grown in confidence greatly and have talked a lot in the staff room about looking at the way they've been doing things in the past and changing things like grouping children more flexibly, how they talk to children and the sort of directions and explanations that they give ... How they approach different areas in Maths. I think it has made everybody think a little more about themselves. The probationary teacher feels she wouldn't have been able to plan for individual children, to differentiate the work as well, if she hadn't had the Standardised Assessment Tests to sort out ... and we really have moved forward in the area of recording/assessment.' (Deputy Head Teacher).

While collaboration between the year 2 teachers had developed well and was beneficial for the development of collaboration between the whole staff there were problems due to limited opportunities for ongoing involvement of all staff and it was recognised that their feelings had been underestimated.

'Co-operation between year 2 teachers developed well. On reflection I think the "feeling of exclusion" by the rest of the staff was overlooked, or at least underestimated by us both.' (Deputy head teacher).

A final comment from one of the year 2 teachers:

'Please don't ever ask me to deprive children of so much learning time or deprive me of job satisfaction again. Having said that I did enjoy the challenge.' (Year 2 teacher A).

TABLE 1	CYCLE ONE JANUARY-MARCH 1991. TEACHER ASSESSMENT PERIOD
January 7th	Staff training day: discuss teaching/learning policy.
11th	Staff meeting: programme meetings for term.
16th	Staff meeting: discuss topic planner recording sheet.
22nd	Staff meeting: books for reading assessment; plan period of assessment. Visit from Moderator.
29th	Staff meeting. Moderator visits deputy/year 2 teachers.
February 4th	Moderation year 2 work (2 teachers and Moderator).
6th	Cluster group meet at Teachers' Centre (year 2 teachers).
11th	Local Education Authority training day: head teacher, deputy and year 2 teachers.
13th	Head teacher and deputy reflect on Local Education Authority training day.
25th	Staff training day with Moderator. Head reports on National Curriculum Key Stage 1 Assessment to governors.
27th	Head teacher and deputy reflect on staff training day.
28th	Cluster group meet at Teachers' Centre (year 2 teachers).
March 5th	Support set meeting.
6th	Local Education Authority training day: head teacher, deputy and year 2 teachers.
11th	Planning: head, deputy, year 2 teachers and Moderator. Head teacher attends National Association of Head Teachers meeting.
13th	Head teacher and deputy reflect on Local Education Authority training day.
18th	Staff training day: input from Moderator about Standardised Assessment Tests for reading; changes agreed to assessment procedures.
19th	Cluster group meeting at Teachers' Centre (year 2 teachers).
20th	Head teacher and deputy reflect on staff training day.
21st	Cluster group at Teachers' Centre (deputy/year 2 teachers).
23rd	Interim validation at Kingston Polytechnic.
27th	Head teacher and deputy reflect on National Curriculum Key Stage 1 teacher assessment period and plan for Standardised Assessment Tests period.
April 19th	Staff meeting (with Local Education Authority Moderator) to review the National Curriculum Key Stage 1 teacher assessment period.

44 *Developing Primary Schools through Action Research*

TABLE TWO	CYCLE TWO APRIL-MAY 1991. Standardised Assessment Tests
27th March	Staff Meeting: plans for Standardised Assessment Tests.
9th April	Meeting with critical friend.
15th	Interim validation meeting attended by deputy, Local Education Authority advisory teacher, critical friend and support set.
16th	Staff Meeting: programme for staff meetings.
17th	(1) Head teacher and deputy discuss arrangements for changes to school assessment procedures; (2) Staff meeting: reporting test results to parents; (3) head teacher reports on Standardised Assessment Tests to governors.
19th	Newsletter to parents about Key Stage 1 Assessment.
22nd	National Association of Head Teachers meeting.
23rd	Head teacher meets support set and critical friend.
24th	(1) Head teacher, deputy and year 2 teachers meet to discuss Standardised Assessment Tests; (2) Parents meeting.
29th	Parents meeting attended by head, deputy and year 2 teachers.
30th	Local Education Authority Moderator moderates Standardised Assessment Tests.
1st May	(1) Head teacher and deputy meet to reflect on Standardised Assessment Tests; (2) Year 2 teacher absent for 2 days.
2nd	Head teacher meets support set and critical friend.
7th	Staff training day: draft Learning/Teaching Policy.
9th	Head teacher and deputy meet to reflect on staff training day.
10th	Negative media coverage of Standardised Assessment Tests.
13th	National Association of Head Teachers meeting.
14th	Head teacher, support set and critical friend meet.
15th	(1) Head teacher and deputy to reflect on Standardised Assessment Tests period and discuss support required for remaining period; (2) Staff meeting: review reading records; plan draft curriculum statements; discuss draft annual reports to parents.
21st	Head teacher meets support set and critical friend.
22nd	Head teacher, deputy and year 2 teachers reflect on Standardised Assessment Tests and data for monitoring.
24th	(1) Standardised Assessment Tests data sent to Local Education Authority; (2) Head teacher meets support set and critical friend.

Evaluating the Implementation of Nation Curriculum Key Stage 1 Assessment Tests

TABLE THREE	CYCLE THREE JUNE - JULY REPORTING TO PARENTS AND EVALUATION OF PROJECT
3rd June	Year 2 teacher absent from school for 2 days.
5th	Head teacher and deputy meet to reflect on project.
10th	Head teacher, deputy and year 2 teachers meet rest of staff to evaluate Standardised Assessment Tests period. Head teacher attends National Association of Head Teachers meeting.
12th	Staff meeting: annual reports to parents discussed. Deputy head teacher begins implementation of Local Education Authority reading rests for year 2 (3 days).
13th	Meeting at Teachers' Centre about National Curriculum Key Stage 1 attended by year 2 teachers.
14th	National Curriculum Key Stage 1 Form sent to Local Education Authority.
17th	Deputy implements Local Education Authority Reading Tests for year 2 (3 days).
19th	Head teacher and deputy prepare report to governors about National Curriculum Key Stage 1 Assessment.
20th	Year 2 teachers prepare annual reports to parents.
24th	Head teacher and year 2 teachers meet to evaluate Standardised Assessment Tests activities.
25th	Head teacher and Local Education Authority Moderator meet to reflect on Standardised Assessment Tests period.

6. Implementing Key Stage 1 Assessment: One Year On

Margaret Follows, Patricia Ede, Alyson Rodway and Suzanne Waites

What follows is a transcript of a meeting held at Spring Park Infant School on Wednesday 20th May. The meeting was attended by the head teacher (MF), the Deputy head teacher (SW), and the two teachers (PE and AR) who had been responsible for carrying out National Curriculum Key Stage 1 Standardised Assessment Testing. The meeting was directed by the head teacher with the purpose of comparing the teachers' recent experience of Key Stage 1 Assessment with that of the previous year. The discussion can be divided into two parts. In part one the teachers discuss how they managed the assessment period and in part two they talk about the Standardised Assessment Tests themselves and what they felt about them.

MF Do you feel that you received the literature in time to prepare for the assessment period?

PE Yes. On the whole it was much earlier than last year... although we did not receive some of the technology literature and some of the administration forms. This year the forms are going to be computerised and it was a bit of an unknown quantity. We did not know how we were going to record the final part of the assessment... but it did not stop us going ahead with the planning. We started the testing without knowing how to deal with the end results.

MF Was the Local Education Authority training sufficient this year? This was the second year of implementing Standardised Assessment Tests so we were given half a day's training as opposed to two days last year.

PE The training was very relevant... but we did not feel as if we were on top of it, even though it was our second year.

AR That is absolutely true... everything that we needed to do... page by page in the book... or on a flip chart with the trainers... it was all clear. Although I felt in command of the situation in putting the test in place... the practice and the teacher assessment... this year... I do feel that there are probably some pages in the handbook that I have not read and could have been relevant that I missed. There hasn't been that time available... especially with other people... we could have done it together... but there have been so many other things we have had to do together, those little things that haven't been covered on the training day.

SW We have managed because we did Standardised Assessment Tests last year, but other teachers will not be trained till after they should have started testing.

MF This year we have not supplemented the time allowed by the Local Education Authority so we have not had extra time in school to catch up with looking at the documents.

PE It has been quite difficult because I haven't been able to meet AR. We have not been able to run together. I have been lagging behind AR. Last year… before or at the end of each day… we could discuss what had happened and then move on together. We have had to work more independently this year. Also… what was missing this year was the opportunity for the four of us to plan together. Last year we had that opportunity at the Teachers' Centre. It was set aside as part of the training… that was missing this time.

MF Has the Local Education Authority Moderator's role been any different this year from last year?

PE Yes, it has… inasmuch as because we were a pilot school last year and things went relatively smoothly, the Moderators have given more time to schools doing it for the first time.

SW The Moderator has not been as much in evidence this year as last year. I do not know whether this is similar to other pilot schools… or whether Moderators have more to cover this year… or trust that we know what we are doing.

AR Moderators have spent the same amount of time watching the Standardised Assessment Test activities this year but last year there was more time to discuss things with them.

PE But the option is there for us to contact the Moderator. I spoke to her on the phone because the Local Education Authority requested that we send in our time charts to give the exact date when we would like the Moderator to come in. Most of us felt that you couldn't predict that far ahead… what you would be doing on a given day. We felt it would be better to work with our Moderator as an individual school. I spoke to her on the phone and she said, 'Let me know if there are any problems… I'll leave it for you to approach me, rather than me keep coming to the school'. So the onus was on us to approach her and we were quite happy with that arrangement.

MF Have there been any concerns this year with the organisation of Standardised Assessment Tests and Teacher Assessment that we couldn't predict from last year?

PE The biggest difficulty has been that the supply cover has not been consistently available. It was a key factor last year… this year we have had to get together after school instead. Fair enough… you expect to… but last year we had a particular day so we could sit down together and talk over important issues. We could resolve it there and then. This year I was unable to get out of the classroom so much and there was no reasonable time available for us to meet.

AR We haven't worked side by side as much as last year... we have had to go our own way at times.

PE By not having the supply cover at the same time, we couldn't work together in school. It meant that we didn't have such long stretches of time working together. It was an odd ten minutes. You need time to reflect and when you are interrupted it is not so valuable as when you can plan the whole session.

MF Our initial plan for both year 2 teachers to be released simultaneously every Friday has not come off... and equally we haven't been able to release SW for part of Friday morning to meet the year 2 teachers on a regular basis if the need arose.

SW We have also had to divert cover to year 2 at the expense of the reception class.

MF Last year we had difficulty with the teacher assessment because our school records didn't provide you with the information that you required. Has that been any easier or as difficult?

AR It has been different. The teacher assessment last year had to be completed at the end of the Spring term prior to the Standardised Assessment Test period. It was two separate entities which presented its own problems. This year they all had to be completed at the same time, which is the end of this week, and this has produced its own problems for me. The last two or three weeks have been problematic and most disruptive for class teaching. I have spent a lot of time trying to update teacher assessment and school records.

PE Last year the teacher assessment was completed in the Spring term. That was finished, then you started Standardised Assessment Tests. All the paperwork was out of the way, then you started testing for 6 weeks. That was a complete entity itself. We drew it together at the end. This year the two have run together. It is problematic. There are bits of this and bits of that.

AR Doing both at the same time is probably to the benefit of the children because the information you have will be more up-to-date... but it is very fiddly. Also... if you do a Standardised Assessment Test activity and use the result for doing your teacher assessment it might save you having to do an assessment on another piece of work. If... say... your child comes out as level 1 on number and really you know they are level 2... it is difficult to know what to do. You have got to make a professional judgement. The teacher assessment can help solve this dilemma.

MF How do you decide which Standardised Assessment Test to give a particular child?

PE It is how well you know the children. It is not difficult.

MF You didn't find it difficult. You selected the level.

AR Yes. That was no problem.

PE That was a great improvement from last year. We had to start by testing children at level 2 last year and ended up having to test at several levels.

For example, L failed at level 2 so I had to test her at level 1 which she passed... as I knew she was capable of level 3 I tested her at that level also and she passed. This year we are allowed to use our own judgement about which level to test. If they fail at level 2 and you know they were capable of better things, you could put them in for level 3. This was more logical.

AR I am not sure about that but that is what it says in the paperwork. It is a strange one, that you can fail at a lower level but pass at a higher level. That is a fault of the activity, because different types of activity ask for different skills... it does not happen often though.

SW It was acknowledged at the training session that teachers should use their professional judgement.

PE Yes. That made a lot of difference this year. Last year you tested till they failed. There's no need to do that this year. If you know they have just got into level 2 and they just about made it, it is pointless testing further. That's the end of it. It's only the teacher who knows whether they are at the beginning of level 2 or in the middle stage or towards the end of level 2 in most things.

MF Have you as class teachers done all the Standardised Assessment Tests with the children or have any of the support staff been able to help you?

PE I have done all mine... except that the support teacher for English as a second language has sat alongside a child as is normal classroom practice.

AR I don't have any ESL children.

PE I would say any staff working with the children, including staff supporting children with special needs, have carried on working in their usual way. They've worked with the same group during Standardised Assessment Tests as they normally do.

MF So they have been a little more involved this year.

PE Oh, yes, but I have administered all the Standardised Assessment Tests.

MF Have you been able to continue classroom routines this year or have you had to adapt any?

AR I've had to adapt and change. I've again lost routines that I have established. At the beginning of last term I introduced a spelling game, which I spent a lot of time preparing. We were just getting into it and the children understood it and were enjoying it, but early on in the Standardised Assessment Tests period we had to stop. I don't think I will get it established this school year.

PE My reading time with the children has been affected, but that happened last year too.

AR Yes. And that has happened with me during the last three weeks whilst I have been completing teacher assessments. I have been spending a lot more time doing that. It's the children who benefit from daily reading that have missed out.

Implementing Key Stage 1 Assessment: One Year On 51

PE   It is the craft work in my class that has been missed because I have been testing in the afternoon.

MF   So again it's the creative and practical activities that have suffered. What about you keeping up with displays of children's work or storing the work that they have done if they have done support sheets?

AR   Yes. I've got wadges of children's work sheets that need to be mounted or put in their folders.

PE   With me I feel the display work in my room has just ground to a halt. There are boards which I should have changed and children's work I should have put up. Our next priority is to hear all the children read regularly, and that has to be done before other things.

MF   I remember last year the location for the Standardised Assessment Tests activities varied slightly. Some were done in the classroom, some were done outside the classroom. Have you had to rethink about that?

AR   Yes... we have... because of the geography of the building... we have not had an extra spare room this year.

MF   What particular activities would you have used that room for?

PE   Activities for sorting, so we can spread out, because the children need to have 20 items to sort. They recommend in the book that you do it as a whole class activity.

MF   Can I just come in here? Have you followed any of the whole class recommendations? Have you done any of the Standardised Assessment Tests as a class activity?

PE   I tried one and it was an absolute disaster. I did it to prove to myself that I wasn't making heavy work of it. It was the number sheet I thought I would try. Inevitably with work sheets you give them out and the children copy each other. You have to say to your children, 'Don't look at your neighbour's work'. At the end of the day, even if you group them in mixed abilities or whatever, you still have children looking at others' work. It was no test. I scrapped it and started again. They say whole class activities cut down the time. It took them 10 minutes to do it, but it was a waste. I felt it was invalid. We didn't try any more like that.

MF   What about the reading? Were you able to integrate the reading Standardised Assessment Tests into the classroom or did you take the children out?

AR   My level 3... I took those out, but level 1 and 2 we did within the class. It depends on how comfortable the teacher working with you feels about you in the classroom... she is responsible for the rest of the children and possible disruptions that may happen with a few children.

I found that I could cut myself off from other class activities, but I am not so sure about the support teachers' feelings, particularly as they are working with children who they don't know very well.

MF   Why did you take level 3 children out for reading?

AR I was doing paperwork at the same time anyway, but level 3 reading involved a child preparing a short passage by themselves and it's quieter. It is the nature of the task that is important.

MF Do you feel your role as a Curriculum Leader has been affected by your involvement with assessment this year? I remember it being a worry last year for you.

AR I try to take it into account when making my year's plan for developing Information Technology in the school. So I planned what I would tackle during this period. I obviously anticipated that I would have less time for Information Technology and helping other staff.

MF Did you feel that other staff avoided coming to you?

AR No.

PE The file on the Special Needs requires updating... and I have not been able to do anything with mathematics with the Nursery Teacher.

MF But mathematics is a shared responsibility. Before Standardised Assessment Tests we were able to release you with the other teacher.

PE It's also the nature of the mathematics development... which includes a lot of paperwork... at the moment and I have reached saturation point with paperwork.

MF Has the rest of the school been affected by Key Stage 1 Assessment?

AR I don't think so. Other people have said that we haven't been so disrupted but the other teachers do not know what is involved in year two.

SW But reception have lost their support teacher to cover the support for PE.

MF Last year we had problems with the behaviour of some children, not only in your classes but around the school.

PE It is difficult to judge, but inevitably children have had their routines changed, which has affected the children, because the children have had to respond to different adults in the classroom. Young children cannot always work independently of the teacher. They need their questions answered. I haven't been able to do that always during the Standardised Assessment Tests period, and the child has gone off and been a nuisance.

AR The demanding children have been affected most.

SW There has been no 'hype' from parents this year. The testing seems to have been totally overlooked.

PE I imagined that the controversy about testing would be an ongoing thing. But I've got a feeling that this is it. We are left to get on with it. There has been no media coverage this year. Not one parent has approached me about it.

MF Is the information you have got about the children from testing useful for you as teachers, or will it be any use for the next year 3 teacher?

AR The teacher assessment will be useful because it's on the children's school record.

PE But the Standardised Assessment Tests for maths and science are being changed for next year, so it does create a problem for Y3 teachers. They'll have to interpret the new Standardised Assessment Tests.

MF We have been working to a deadline. You have kept to it. How much good will have you given it? How much extra time do you think you have given to keep the programme going? Has it encroached on your family life?

AR Yes. Since the Easter holidays when I've been doing teacher assessments. The last four weeks have been very pressurised, even though the time consuming Standardised Assessment Tests activities were done last term.

PE You've got to bring strands together at the same point. That is the assessment and the Standardised Assessment Tests. Last year they were separate.

MF Have you spent much extra time preparing for the Standardised Assessment Tests activities?

PE Not really. We use all the classroom resources. When we did the sorting the children collected things on walks. So it was part of their learning.

MF You spent a long time collating the data. How much time?

PE I spent 8 hours on the Saturday. It brings all the information together.

AR I have been able to do some of this in my extra release time, and I've completed my assessment record book as I've gone along. That's not been as easy for PE... she's done it at home. She hasn't always had the support in the classroom to be able to complete the assessment data alongside the Standardised Assessment Test activity.

PE Yes. If you are testing with no help, that ten minutes just for paperwork is too much. You've got to come back to it later.

AR The support teacher also takes the children off for assembly or play time so you can do the paperwork. You can write the results straight away for the four children you have been previously testing. It is completed much quicker. That worked very well this year.

MF So now you need to transfer the information onto the forms for the Local Authority. Is there still going to be enough time on Friday to do this?

PE Yes, I think so.

MF Let's look at the nature of the Standardised Assessment Tests activities themselves. How much choice has there been for you? Have you had any options about which Standardised Assessment Tests you use?

AR We chose one optional maths and one optional science.

MF So you've had compulsory maths, science and English. What about time taken for each Standardised Assessment Test activity? Do you feel this year that you have been able to complete each activity in an appropriate time for the children?

AR I think they've been all right this year.

PE The number of things you have had to test has been reduced. The length of time has not been over stressful on the children. Last year some went on too long. They've been broken down into quite small units. But the time allowed for administering the Standardised Assessment Tests has not been improved by whole class activities. That's been no help at all.

MF Most of our children are level 1 or level 2. Do you feel that Standardised Assessment Tests will get more complex, therefore more lengthy for level 3 and level 4?

AR Yes, definitely.

MF So I need to try and get some feedback from schools with those children in.

PE It's an accumulative thing. The higher you go the more you have to test.

AR For writing level 4 you have to write a letter or a story.

MF What about the fairness of the test this year?

AR This year the children have tended to work independently of other influences. Level 2 instant recall of number facts I think is unfair because the children have never been put in that situation before... where they have a small time limit or need to know the answers straight away. I think that put pressure on some children and flummoxed them.

PE Imagine trying to do that as a class activity. Checking that nobody is using fingers and toes to count.

AR I was present at the spelling activity which like last year I set as a separate activity from the story, because I felt that it limited their creativity. There was absolute horror from some of the children when they knew they couldn't use dictionaries to help them. But when they got used to the idea, they just got on with it. I think I did that one with about half the class.

PE I had two children who did not produce anything, both very sensitive children, who need coaxing from an adult. It is impossible for them if they have no resource to help them.

MF Are there any specific Standardised Assessment Tests worthy of a mention?

AR They did change the story writing this year. Last year the children could retell a story... they didn't say yes or no to that this year. Don't know why they haven't said you can't, but last year they actually almost encouraged it. Last year if they hadn't said you can get them to retell a story, we may well have thought we can't do that because it is not the same as creating their own story.

PE   We were surprised when the Moderator said we could do it. AR's class actually did a completely creative story after some practical work they had done. My class did a retell of a story, which was fine for me to assess till I got to level 3, and then the more able children were disadvantaged. They were retelling a story sequence of events perhaps not using the extended, connective vocabulary they would have done if it had been all out of their imagination.

MF   That would be an interesting activity to follow through with more advanced children, or another school perhaps.

PE   If I was doing it again, I would use a creative story.

AR   My level 3 child was in fact retelling a story. It was Rumpelstiltskin that we'd seen 3 months beforehand with the theatre group, so the words were hers, rather than words provided by a book.

AR   The handwriting is an interesting one.

PE   It's to do with ascenders and descenders... for that we taught to the test. In the last three months we have been using lined paper to show descenders and ascenders. That's because it is a very specific skill. Last year my children's handwriting was quite sophisticated but the descenders let them down because they had not been writing on lines... it would be quite interesting to hear from other schools and other teachers here.

MF   Perhaps we need to look again at the school's handwriting policy?

AR   But I think it is a developmental thing. We could include it with the variety of materials that are available on writing tables.

MF   We also tried the optional spelling test for level 2 and level 3 children.

SW   That was an activity we decided to do with small withdrawal groups administered by the Deputy Head.

PE   Yes, we opted in. It was mandatory for level 3 and level 4 but optional for level 2. We did it in groups of 5 or 6 so that it was quiet. We used the medical room.

SW   They had their own tables... they couldn't look at each other's work. It was a very strange format on the paper, but the children adapted to it very well. The teacher read the passage, and the children wrote the words that were missing into the passage. They listened to the passage first and then I re-read the passage and stopped at each missing word.

MF   Could we have done it as a whole class activity?

SW   Yes... but it was inappropriate for our children because it would be difficult to interpret the result. The first thing our children did even in a small group was to look at each other's work. That's because we encourage the children to work collaboratively and talk together.

MF   What did they think of the actual story?

SW   It was totally inappropriate as it mentioned unfamiliar sports such as squash. It was a very middle class story.

PE   But it did include some of the teaching strategies, that is word families that we had been using, bearing in mind that we did not know the text.

AR   Diagnostically it was quite useful. You could spot the gaps.

MF   I think I have come to the end of my questions. Is there anything else you would like to add?

PE   Just that we were glad it was finished.

MF   What about a possible organisation for Standardised Assessment Tests next year? Would you both consider being Y2 teachers again if required to?

AR   Our school records are now complete. It has taught me to be more aware of key things in school records during that year 2 period. The need to up-date them more regularly. The importance of having ongoing assessment rather than half termly records. Pick different subjects out of smaller topics. Yes, I would be quite happy to tackle it again next year. But extra subjects are coming on line.

PE   I must say that the message given out by the press that the pencil and paper tests, the class activities are easier, is wrong. You just cannot do it that way. You have got to do them in small groups.

SW   It is worthless doing them in class groups. The results would not mean a thing. The press has given a false impression. That kind of work is an inappropriate form of testing for 7 year olds.

MF   Do you think there will be any value in sharing your expertise in another year group, maybe to prepare year 1 for year 2?

PE   Yes. It could be a distinct advantage for either of us to move to year 1 for the development of the preparation for the Standardised Assessment Tests procedures to channel them into certain topics. Also other teachers should have the experience of year 2. It is important to keep it a whole school issue. I'm thinking of it both from the children's point of view and the staff development.

MF   Thank you all for being so helpful.

7. Who's Testing Who's Testing What?

Barbara Abbey and Valerie Martin

During the great debates about testing prior to the widespread abolition of the 11+ it was whispered with some irony that intelligence was what intelligence tests measured. Can the same criticism be made of the Standardised Assessment Tests that are part of the National Curriculum reforms of the late 1980s and early 1990s? Perhaps of more importance, are we clear about whom and what these tests are designed to measure?

As two teachers in the thick of National Curriculum Key Stage 1 Assessment we are well placed to evaluate what has happened so far: one of us being the teacher in charge of the pupils undergoing assessment; and the other the head teacher and therefore chief Standardised Assessment Test setter in our outer London primary school. The centrality of our experience has also been confirmed by the School Examinations and Assessment Council and we have been invited **with the permission of our authority** to participate in the evaluation of the statutory assessment 1991 **and** 1992!

The chain of events leading to the implementation of the Standardised Assessment Tests in our school in 1991 is reproduced in Table 1. These events seemed at points to merge into each other because we found the processes of assimilation and accommodation painful due to the volume and speed of change. The information overload was delivered by the overworked postman and clarified by the equally overworked advisory teachers. Invariably the national press claimed access to information about matters on which schools had been given no information and stirred anxieties amongst both teachers and parents.

Our response to the questions posed by the questionnaire from the School Examination and Assessment Council provides a useful framework for airing some of our concerns about Standardised Assessment Testing (see chapter 7 for a more detailed analysis of a response to the School Examination and Assessment Council questionnaire).

The first area for response was to do with inservice training, planning and time management. How well? Who trained? How many days? How much time with your family did you give up? This was the gist of the questioning.

But who is being tested?

The Local Education Authority?

The teacher?

The next area under scrutiny was classroom management. We were asked about managing to maintain a balanced curriculum for the whole of the class during the standardised assessment period. There were boxes to fill in to tell that the class (all 22 of them) had the additional help of the head teacher, one other teacher, and a good final year teaching student; but

58 *Developing Primary Schools through Action Research*

Table 1	Events Leading to Implementation of Standardised Assessment Tests
December 1990	Meetings with colleagues in other schools to plan timetables and discuss the paperwork that had reached us by then. Fit that with the schema initiated by the national press!
January 1991	Visit from the Local Education Authority advisor for Standardised Assessment Testing (formerly the language support/advisory teacher Sharon, wearing her new hat which had been rapidly designed on the hoof) to discuss even more paperwork, negotiate meaning, help planning and support our ever positive staff.
March 1991	A full day training session with other colleagues; this cancelled one of the five inservice training days that are allocated to individual schools to implement their school development plans.
	Selected by School Examination and Assessment Council as part of a sample of schools to evaluate Standardised Assessment Testing.
	On our own to 'do' the awful deeds.
	Moderation visit from the Local Education Authority Moderator (formerly the ever helpful Standardised Assessment Test advisor Sharon, with an even newer hat).
	Results dispatched (under protest) to the Local Education Authority and to the School Examination and Assessment Council. (Quite a good range of cognitive skills and time was required in the collation of the scoring).
	Questionnaire returned to School Examination and Assessment Council.
	The teachers return to teaching.

despite all this our tick had to go in the 'not at all' box in answer to the balanced curriculum question. That, coupled with the fact that we were forced to own up to spending 45 hours more than usual on preparation and planning during the Standardised Assessment Test period, did little to promote us as competent classroom managers and did not raise our self esteem.

Who is being tested?
The teacher?

With regard to the activities themselves on a scale of one to five for their approach to the curriculum, manageability, interest, enjoyment and suitability, we found great difficulty in moving away from the median satisfactory score.

Had we teachers failed again?

It took some time for children to enter into the equation. One could hardly believe that they were to be active participants in this procedure. Should we do all this to them? This was certainly a worry of parents who failed to comprehend the fairness of a test that assumed that two children (born eleven months apart) could reasonably be expected to be at the same developmental stage at the ripe old age of six. If the initiators of the tests had had the benefit of the National Curriculum (**science attainment target 1, level 3**) when they were at school they would be able to distinguish between a 'fair' and an 'unfair' test. As it happened parents were left trying to understand a procedure that, using the same scoring method, and testing children's ability to walk, would say that children who walk at nine months of age score three, those who walk at twelve months of age score two and those who take longer to reach that milestone could score one (or worse still W - working towards).

Is that a fair test?

Were children totally reactive in the assessment or were they proactive? There certainly was not much scope for idiosyncratic approaches but then, could that not be said about all forms of testing? However, it certainly led us to question if teaching could still be considered an art or a craft or rather a labour or professional activity (depending of course on your perspective of 'professional'). There is no set of generic skills for teaching but teacher action, contributing towards effective teaching such as: climate, planning, management, subject knowledge, act of teaching and interpersonal relationships, is still essential to us at our school and we felt that the assessment called for robotic type stimulus and response action.

Is this a test of teaching methods?

There was no time to develop the exciting things that children were discovering through the Standardised Assessment Tests themselves. A good example is that 'floating and sinking' Standardised Assessment Test. The children who discovered that a banana floated on Monday, Tuesday and Wednesday but sank on Thursday and Friday could have investigated the ripeness of bananas and the relationship of ripeness to floating and sinking perhaps. Or was it simply the fact that the banana got waterlogged? Perhaps all bananas float for three days a week! Also we, the teachers, have managed to cope with life very nicely thank you up to our ripe old age of...... without having to find out if an onion floats or sinks. For those of you who need to know more, we have it on good authority that it depends on how you cut the onion. We have just been complaining about the lack of time to explore the potential of these Standardised Assessment Tests. This year's Standardised Assessment Tests have been simplified so that teachers can go on a three day week along with the bananas. Perhaps they could be simplified even more and teachers could just teach the answers to the questions.

Is this a test of educational philosophy?
What is different this year then?.....
What is simpler?.....

Who is it simpler for?.....

Marrying the two Standardised Assessment Test year attempts together we ask: 'Is it for better or for worse this year?'

For the teacher the assessment takes less time to complete which means that we can get on with the job of teaching instead of testing. This must mean that it is better.

For the teacher it takes less time to prepare. After all it was a time consuming business finding all these 'natural' objects to float and sink. This year instead of having to gather things together we were presented with a worksheet with a picture of a cupboard on it with things inside it for us to look at. (**Maths 12 level one**, however, did ask us to collect 20 objects for each child.)

Maths 3 Part C: Fruit and Vegetables required that the children wrote their answers to the mental arithmetic questions on the strawberry or on the plum: *'Please, Miss, I can't see a plum. I've only got a tomato left.'* The five seconds permitted to answer the question were swallowed up in debate of the fruit issue and little time was left for the mental arithmetic. For the child it was less fun, more boring, more confusing and more threatening as it was seen as a test. This **must** mean that it was worse for the children.

Certainly the tests have been made 'simpler' to reduce the teacher workload but by doing so more stress has been created in the children.

For the parents it is just as bewildering as last year. 'What will they do with the results?' ask the parents.

'Well,' said we, trying as ever to be positive, 'they will know if the National Curriculum is working. They will know if teachers are getting appropriate initial training. They will know if teachers are getting appropriate in-service training. They will know if schools are good schools. They will know which areas of the curriculum, which schools and which teachers require extra financial resources to help them do their job better'.

*** So that 'appropriate' financial resources are given in the future it may well be wise to reinforce in children (while they are children) the notion that schools are second rate institutions with second hand furniture as quoted in **Maths 12**.

> **To set up a new classroom, these are some of the things your school will need:**   1 carpet - second hand
> 15 tables - second hand
> 30 chairs for children - second hand.

What message is this giving to children? ***

'Well', said the parents, trying as ever to be positive, 'can they not find this out another way? Why test my child if this is what they want to find out?'

GOOD QUESTION.........

PART THREE: DEVELOPING THE WHOLE SCHOOL CONTEXT FOR NATIONAL ASSESSMENT

8. Observing pupils and listening to parents: aspects of a primary school policy on pupil assessment

Janet Mulholland

The work for this project began by my identifying a school need to address the question of pupil assessment. It seemed evident to me that the school recording and pupil assessment system was not best suited to the new national requirements. This was a prominent concern for many schools in 1990/91, not just my own.

Much of my early planning and reconnaissance was concerned with drawing out from this far reaching subject a specific line of research which would have most value to the school. The school is a voluntary aided primary school of about 370 pupils aged 3+ to 9+ years, serving an urban community of one religious denomination. My role as head teacher was a new one, although as I had been deputy head teacher at the school since January 1990, I had a reasonable though not long term knowledge of the organisation. Most of the pupils belong to the local parish or the three surrounding ones. There are 18 members of staff, 11 of whom are full time teachers with responsibility for a class. Classes are large, all but two containing 35 pupils.

Unfortunately the school governors were unable to fill the vacant post of deputy head teacher for the duration of the project, and the role was held on an acting basis renewed termly. The acting deputy head teacher became an invaluable consultant and supporter and was the natural choice as my critical friend.

Pupil assessment was an area of concern. Whilst I felt a high standard of teaching was evident, much of the record keeping had not kept pace with change. Teachers had a good understanding of the pupils in their class but relied too much on verbal reporting to pass this information on. **Real** evidence of achievement was not readily available. In 1991 the spotlight was going to be on the seven year old classes with the introduction of standard assessment tests. I therefore felt I must highlight the particular situation regarding this crucial Key Stage 1 group.

At the beginning of the project year the two relevant classes both contained 35 pupils. Both the year 2 teachers, one experienced and one probationary, were planning to leave the school in December 1990 and July 1991 respectively. In response to an initiative I had planned in the previous academic year following an inservice training day, the school had become associated with a project concerned with a systematic observation and recording of the 'whole child' at entry to school and in the pre National Curriculum years. I had applied for myself and one other member of staff to take part. In the event two other members of staff, the nursery class teacher and a reception class teacher, had a strong desire to take part. We agreed that I would give up my own place but would be kept fully up to date with the course.

The local context was one of much change educationally and politically. After many years, a different party had achieved majority at local elections in 1990, and new relationships were being forged between Local Government and the Local Education Authority; financially, serious cuts were affecting schools as a result of local difficulties. Unfortunately these problems were not eased before April 1991 when schools were given a fully delegated budget for the first time. Primary schools in particular were seriously underfunded. Problems were especially bad for schools like ours whose actual salary costs were above the Local Education Authority's average, a consequence of having many staff at the top of pay scales. Budget delegation entailed much preparation and training at both local and school level at the very time that curriculum initiatives were in need of considerable attention. The situation was further compounded by many of the local head teachers being newly appointed, particularly in my own voluntary aided group where only one established head teacher remained. Thus there were many pressures and stresses operating on all staff members at that time. The context for the introduction of standard assessment tests could have been more auspicious. The situation was not made easier by the fact that a time lag occurred between information being given about pupil assessment and the establishment of local training and consultancies for staff; whilst specific information about requirements concerning standard assessment tests for Key Stage 1 were not present until even later.

Local Education Authority information concerning reports to parents which had to be introduced in conjunction with pupil assessment was also late arriving but was established by April 1991. This was in advance of similar Department of Education and Science recommendations. Department of Education and Science circulars 8/90 and 9/90 together with the School Examination and Assessment Council Assessment publications became the mainstay of information about National Assessment, and provided support for the establishment of our observation assessment project. It was stated that Key Stage 1 Assessment would be carried out in the spring and summer of 1991. The results would be compiled from both teacher assessment activities and Standardised Assessment Tests. A specific formula to merge these results was outlined and the time scale for completing the process was laid down. Regulations for reporting to parents in the summer term were set out and the differences between open and private school records addressed. The Standardised Assessment Test pack was not available to anyone until the end of February 1991. At this point it was also available freely to parents from stationers in most high streets.

My belief in the importance of good observation skills and full assessment made me more critically aware of the values that underpinned my action. These can be summarised in this way:

1. the belief that the **form** of assessment of pupils is important in order to ensure that progress takes place;
2. the belief that assessment should be part of the child's learning process; it should not impede that process or direct it;
3. the belief that assessment should be about the whole child and not narrowed to specific pre-determined National Curriculum attainment targets;
4. the belief that assessment should be **useful** in that it effectively informs educators as they review how individual needs are being met;
5. the belief that an ongoing assessment, backed by well evidenced records, is most appropriate for pupils at the primary level;
6. the belief that the development of the observational skills of staff are crucial to the assessment process;
7. the belief that parents must take part in the assessment process from the earliest opportunity and know that their perceptions of the child are highly valued; and
8. the belief that pupils have much to contribute in their own self assessment.

My initial aims reflected the reconnaissance nature of my first cycle of research. They were broad in scope and reflected the concerns I had at that time. They also enabled me to fulfil the criteria I had set myself: ensuring that the focus I chose was of real value to the school.

This **first cycle** was a cycle of 'anticipation' where information about the exact nature of National Assessment requirements was awaited. I used this period to involve the whole staff in a review of existing assessment practices. Underpinning this was the intention that this review would result in setting whole school priorities which would be reflected in the school development document, and which would guide part of our forward planning for in-service training.

Once I had completed this first cycle, my focus was defined and affirmed. My own values directed me firmly towards the importance of sound well-evidenced records as a basis for assessment, and further, that observation of the 'whole' child is the only way for truly accurate assessment. This must include input from parents who have the expert knowledge on each child.

With this as the guiding focus, I entered the **second cycle** of my research. This cycle was to prove the busiest and probably the most interesting from my point of view. The focus of our work was shared with the schools assigned inspector, the early years inspector and with an early years advisory teacher. Another member of staff became involved exploring the use of observation in establishing achievement in National Curriculum terms. During this time information was shared and discussed between the participating staff, the deputy head teacher and myself. Planning was exciting and largely a co-operative concern. In management terms it was difficult to separate planning and action as the two were interwoven; ideas were tried out, monitored and reflected upon in the light of experience and external pressures. Feedback from various sources including interviews with parents was most useful and informed future planning for enhancing teacher observation.

INTERVIEWS WITH PARENTS

These interviews with parents gave much information which enabled teachers to understand many of the children's observed behaviours better. At the very least parents were supportive of our efforts to include them. Many were very enthusiastic and expressed gratitude for the opportunity to come in and put their 'side of the picture'. As one parent said:

> 'Whatever you do, don't stop these interviews. I have had three other children through this school and was never given the chance to explain what I felt made them tick and what their needs were. I feel I know Mrs. Anon now and that I can talk to her when I need to. I think she knows much more about where my son is coming from...'

Another said,

> 'Thank you for making this time for us. We really want to do all that we can for Janet and it's good to see that you care enough to find out all that you can about Janet as an individual person....'

And another,

> 'I always used to worry about coming up to the school to see the teacher. Now I feel much better about it. The teachers always seemed to do all the talking. Sometimes it didn't sound like my kids at all....'.

In some cases information was divulged which had not been previously known to the school even where older siblings had been in school for some time. Frequently this cast a whole new light on a concern. I must underline that this was not as a result of probing questioning, which was not our brief, but of supplying a time for parents to relate what they perceived as important to the understanding of their child.

Only two parents really did attempt to use this time to focus heavily on academic matters and impress on us how 'brilliant' their children were. One of these also outlined fixed notions of what the school should do with their child. Both of these were encouraged to develop the view into a wider consideration of the whole child during the course of the 30 minutes. Ultimately a more rounded picture of the child and the purposes of schooling was established. These interviews were particularly valuable to the reception class teacher as she now had a better awareness of parental attitudes and expectations.

Not one adverse comment was made by parents at the time or, as far as I can ascertain, since, regarding the procedure. Only one set of parents declined to come despite being offered several different times and dates, whilst a significant number of parents made efforts to ensure that both partners attended, many of these having made special arrangements with employers to be free. This successful beginning allowed us to enter the extension of these interviews to the nursery section, with confidence.

A programme of home visits for children about to join the nursery class was also initiated in this second cycle of research. The visits went very smoothly and were an immediate success. The nursery teacher and nursery nurse popped into school as and when their appointments allowed. 'It's all going very well indeed. It's so useful to us and to the parents who are really delighted' (nursery teacher). 'I knew it would be helpful, but it's so much more than that. We already have an understanding of the children that might have taken a term or more to establish before' (nursery nurse). 'It wasn't just the first few families. Everyone has been so pleased and so supportive. We must keep this practice up for future intakes of children. There is no comparison between this relationship with families and what we had before.' (nursery nurse).

WHOLE CHILD OBSERVATION

Also in this period we began to pilot a method of whole child observation which we considered would be very helpful in informing the assessment procedure that was due to be installed. There were several problems associated with this. We all agreed that in the first few instances observations were difficult to complete. Diversions in particular were difficult to ignore. We agreed that stopping at the designated time was often hard. Frequently we became too interested to see what would happen next. We found that the children were usually aware that they were being watched. We were not able to make notes without arousing curiosity, either of the subject child, or others in the area, or both. The Reception teacher even had offers to draw in her special book! We decided that if the children got used to the sight of staff frequently making notes it may not bother them eventually. An hypothesis yet to be tested!

It was important to observe children in a variety of situations and on different days. This was highlighted for me in a series of observations that I undertook on one boy who was bright, intelligent and co-operative in most situations but when crossed exhibited quite different characteristics. Had I relied on the evidence of two of the observations alone this would not have been picked up. We discussed the need to continue to observe children to help sustain evidence of the success or failure of any intervention procedures. This was important to highlight changes or progress in the passage of time. I believe that knowing the children well is not achieved by a one off investigation but by a constantly reviewed and renewed process.

Already we were sufficiently convinced that regular observations of pupils was an essential part of understanding them and very necessary for appropriate planning to meet individual needs. This scheme had given encouraging results in terms of the children and their teachers, but also had the effect of changing the role of the participant teachers as they gradually took on greater ownership of the scheme. By the end of this cycle of research they had (rightly) negotiated to remove my practical involvement from the project with regard to the piloting of child observations. This coincided with the beginning of the Local Education Authority sponsored training in preparation for the standard assessment tests and marked the transition point for moving to **Cycle three** of the research.

This cycle was in some ways a breathing space for those staff directly involved. They continued to develop skills in observing pupils and to consolidate ideas. Some sharing and passing on of ideas occurred sometimes formally and at other times informally. Methods of charting observations were discussed and tried out particularly with regard to the evidenced attainment. The move to extend the observational scheme to the whole school was put temporarily on 'hold' and the whole school preparation for year two assessment was allowed to take precedence. Whilst I was giving priority to managing the introduction of Standardised Assessment Tests, I also wanted to keep in touch regularly with developments in observing pupils and to encourage the reception class and nursery class teachers in their scheme.

The reception class teacher was pleased to have 'more time to practise and to prepare before feeding back to the staff. It will give us far more confidence'. The nursery class teacher admitted that she felt that what we were doing was the answer but was not sure that she had practised the observational methods enough herself yet to explore them with colleagues, and thus also appreciated having a little more time for reflection and practice.

The general feeling was that the whole staff were getting jittery over the assessment question. It was a frequent topic of conversation in the staff room, and each time the topic emerged, fresh worries were revealed. This made it even more imperative to support the whole staff in their National Assessment training and preparation, even though this meant that some initiatives that had been planned for the extending of parental involvement and whole child observation were temporarily put on 'hold'.

Reflections upon what might make the scheme more effective continued, however. A new reception class teacher was initiated into the methods and approaches of our observation scheme and parental interviews continued with the new reception class parents. These parents were just as positive as the first group had been and many seemed more clued up, having apparently spoken to friends with pupils in the first reception class. Parents certainly settled down more quickly at the interview. Three parents brought along a list with them as they were determined to leave nothing out! This did seem to give credence to the reception class teacher's theory that parents would begin to respond in a quicker manner once they were *au fait* with the system. I found it interesting that so many of these mentioned that they had spoken to other parents about the meetings: the explanation in the appointment letter was obviously not sufficient. I added this factor to the summary of parental responses.

The children did appear to have lost initial interest in the note taking but did still seem to have a sixth sense when they were the subject of observation. Occasionally this led to a display behaviour pattern but this tended to be short lived.

The information that the teachers gained from their structured observations of the new group of children ranged from the interesting to the revealing. Sometimes evidence was produced backing the teachers' unsubstantiated feelings. Sometimes surprises had been thrown up. The reception class teacher cited one example where a seemingly bright and busy child was observed on several occasions doing little but flitting from group to group. She appeared to be involved in the action, but was actually very passive in the centre of each activity. Both reception class and nursery class teachers were firmly convinced about the value of their observational practice, and were committed to extending the number of children whom they systematically observed.

The year 1 teacher was also experimenting with different types of observation. Usually she attempted to highlight one or two attainment targets in her observations. Frequently however she found that the targets she watched for were in fact cross-curricular even if the task set was quite specific (speaking and listening skills for instance were a regular feature). She did feel, however, that in order to be sure that certain attainment targets had been met, there was a maximum number of factors that a teacher could observe in any one group at any one time. This teacher had been experimenting with grid methods of recording and had put together a format that she had found to work well. This grid was later accepted as a useful pro-forma by staff and was adopted for trial purposes.

This cycle was most useful. It had served most of its planned functions and had allowed 'the team' more time to build up competence and confidence. New issues and questions were being raised that would allow further elaboration and involvement of staff (for example, whether it should always be the class teacher who is the observer), and we had made real progress with regard to the attainment observations.

However... during this period the Standardised Assessment Tests hysteria rose up in every corner of the Local Education Authority. The media made sure that staff could not go home and simply forget about it. Altogether it was a frustrating and debilitating time while we waited to see **the pack**. My main task was to keep staff calm and offer as much support as possible to year 2 teachers. Subject co-ordinators were concentrating on these classes too, working alongside the year 2 teachers. The project could not have been extended at this time and I became increasingly glad that I had not attempted to do so.

The **fourth cycle** was a moving on stage in the project. Planning was to become a major event to ensure effective feedback to all staff about the ways in which the attainment observations had been working. The main objective underpinning this was to generate whole school involvement in the observational programme. Draft documentation was drawn up and plans were set for much wider trials and investigations. The co-operative and enthusiastic support of my 'basic' team of co-researchers was extremely important here. By this stage there was no doubt that they were fulfilling their role of researchers of the attainment observation process.

This phase of our work took place amongst a general feeling of anger and inadequacy with regard to assessment. Effective planning had been precluded by not having received sight of the Standardised Assessment Tests as a complete package until a much later date, and several staff raised worries about teachers in general taking the blame for the effects of such blatantly rushed and overburdening assessment procedures having been imposed upon us. There was also a very real concern for the year 2 teachers and pupils, so much so that we felt that they needed safe-guarding and agreed, against our general principles, to concentrate support cover in year 2 classes for the half term in which the Standardised Assessment Tests were to take place.

I found it most helpful at this highly emotional time to refer staff back to the Local Education Authority statement made in October 1990 supporting as top priorities:

> 'Pupil learning and pupil and staff well being... Assessment must come second to those considerations'.

It became important to remind staff that one of the most useful things we could do would be to update our ongoing practice and as far as possible make it do the job for us in the future. During staff discussions there was unanimous agreement that we should address internal whole school assessment/record keeping issues and try to establish helpful practice and policy. It was clearly important now to address pupil assessment in school as a priority. Parental input procedures were going well and were valued in the lower school, but I felt that unless staff voluntarily picked up the lead of the reception and nursery class teachers, then a full extension of the practice to the whole school ought only to be considered at a later date. A planned inservice training day allowed us to share and plan for a whole school policy on assessment.

There was unanimous agreement amongst staff regarding attainment targeted observation strategies. Great interest was expressed in the experiences of the year 1 teacher and there was general approval to try out the grid system for recording. An initial target concerning numbers of observations to be attempted, and the main emphasis of these, was agreed although it would be reviewed in the autumn term. We agreed that year 2 teachers would not take part this term as they were already overburdened and would both be leaving school in July.

Despite a full and informative feedback by the reception class teacher and nursery class teacher there was mixed reaction to the idea of **whole child** observations. The first reaction of a senior member of staff:

> 'I think they are totally unnecessary, although I can see that they are useful in the nursery and reception classes where the families and pupils might be new'

had quite an impact and led to a lively discussion. The reception class teachers and the nursery class teacher were able to argue an opposite case and pointed out that they had begun with an open mind and had only been convinced by practice. The year 1 teacher told staff that she had discovered several surprises which disproved some of her pre-conceptions in observing attainment and she wondered if this might not also be the case with the overall impressions about some pupils. I suggested that we resolved our differences by **having a go** (to use the reception class teacher's jargon) and a half term trial excluding year 2 was readily agreed.

The in-service training day proved to be very rigorous and exhausting but most productive. The deputy head teacher felt:

'It was a full, frank and fair day approached in a spirit of goodwill. Through information, group work and discussion the staff had moved on enormously.'

and added

'Everyone has gone home tired tonight but with a positive outlook....'

One of the scribes allowed me to record her remark:

'I could feel a strong team spirit today. Everyone was trying to do something to get a helpful system in place.'

In order to manage this situation of change I was clear that I needed to keep an open forum approach and, hopefully, establish the credibility of observation practice. I did not want a system which was perceived to be imposed nor a system which was seen as irrelevant to current need. I knew that it was my co-researchers who held the key roles in demonstrating the effectiveness of observation in the classroom situation. It was important therefore to plan carefully with them and encourage them in making a substantial input. There is no doubt in my mind that this was a particularly important factor in the establishment of trials on whole child observations throughout the school.

We did not address a policy on the extension of parent interviews on this day but both the home visits and reception interviews have been well celebrated by all who have taken part. So much so, that with the updating of requirements for written reports for parents I envisage wide support for the spirit of these parental interviews to be carried on in the older classes.

By the summer of 1991 the project had progressed and the first wave of Standardised Assessment Tests was completed. A review of what had happened in the four cycles of my research during the year reveals that:

- whole child observations had been established on a trial basis as a means of evidencing specific attainment;
- pre-nursery home visits were now a part of school policy with financial support for the scheme written into the 1991/2 school budget;
- a new approach to initial parent meetings was now in place, where parents were encouraged to add observations on their own child into the school records;
- all staff were participating in the formulation of draft policy documents regarding on-going assessment and records of achievement.

This study arose out of a need to improve, enrich and inform our pupil records in order that they would serve teachers better in their understanding and assessment of pupils. It involved developing my management techniques in the introduction of modified and unified assessment practice, and it has entailed my looking into my own activities and developing personal research skills as well as involving a review of the changes brought about in my school as a consequence of my activities. It is a personal study relevant to a very specific set of circumstances; but I would claim that the climate of collaboration and consultation that has been central to my studies has allowed us as a staff to look towards positive and creative ways of effective diagnostic assessment of pupils. Whilst this process is by no means complete, the strategies that are currently in place will help to make sure that assessment is used to ensure progress in children's learning, and to facilitate our assessment activities with regard to Standardised Assessment Tests and teacher assessment. In conclusion I would like to emphasise the developmental quality of my work and my belief that significant changes have been generated. These should be seen in the context of a wider management role at a time of many national and local initiatives.

9. Developing and Implementing Records of Achievement to Meet the Needs of Children with Special Educational Needs

Gail Larkin

I have been deputy head teacher of a first school for the past three years. The school (which I will call my parent school) is one of the largest schools in my Borough, with a roll of approximately 420 children aged 3-8 years. The staff consists of the head teacher plus fourteen full time and three part time teachers. This research began, however, in September 1990 when I was seconded to a special school for children with emotional and behaviour difficulties. The school was without a head teacher and during my one term secondment I worked closely with the deputy head teacher who became acting head teacher. At that time there were only twelve children in the special school. There were three full-time class teachers, two part-time teachers and music and movement therapists. Most of the teachers had been at the school for less than one year. I had been seconded from my parent school for one term and part of my brief was to facilitate the implementation of the National Curriculum and assessment in the special school (which I will call my host school).

In my parent school I had already started work on developing records of achievement which I believed would be essential in the light of the changing assessment regulations being brought about by the new National Curriculum. Through this work it had become obvious to me that we were not meeting the needs of all children in the mainstream school, and in particular children with special educational needs. This insight was crucial to my thinking when the question of assessment and record-keeping came under review in my host school. Traditional methods of assessment presented problems for special educational needs children in the special school context. They also presented difficulties for the children with special educational needs in main stream schooling. Thus the first stage of this project became associated with developing an appropriate policy on records of achievement for children with special educational needs.

RESEARCH STRATEGY

When I began to consider my overall plan of action, I reflected on previous experiences that I had in managing change. In my experience I have found that the most successful 'ingredients' for the implementation of change and problem-solving have been:-

1. to encourage active participation, support and co-operation from as many areas and people as possible;
2. to work 'in situ', that is, in the context in which the problem is diagnosed;
3. to work systematically and slowly, taking small steps rather than going for grandiose movement;
4. to improve communication within the schools and with outside agencies and to inform and involve other interested contributors;
5. to consider critically my own practice and establish good practice in my own actions; and
6. to make myself as fully informed as possible about the area under consideration.

It seemed essential that the approach that I used had the capacity to incorporate all these 'ingredients'. My experience of action research suggested that it was the appropriate approach and therefore the design of the study follows a pattern of discussions, planning and the trialling of new ideas (that is, acting, observing and recording, and then reflecting on what has happened and making plans for the next stage of the programme).

A driving force behind my choice of approach was my belief that the most important reason for conducting research was to change current practice and encourage professional development. This is summed up for me in Whitehead and Foster's writing (1984) when they say that:

> 'Educational research should be ....to improve the relationship between educational theory and professional development. We take educational theory to be a kind of theory which can arise from, and in turn generate, explanations for the educational development of individuals in a form which is open to public testing'.

Action research is concerned with 'in situ' improvements of current educational practices. For me the choice of adopting an action research approach was governed by its practicality and its relevance for the practising teacher. It is both situational and participatory: principles that I held very strongly and wished both to implement in my own professional practice and to facilitate in the practice of my colleagues. Of particular importance to me was the fact that this way provided strategies for me as a teacher and researcher that enabled me to change the practices that negated the values which I held about teaching and learning.

Action research places particular stress on the way in which action is monitored and evaluated in order to inform subsequent action. Strategies for collecting data about action need to be rigorous and its analysis and evaluation need to be systematic and explicit. Undoubtedly the most beneficial strategy for me was the 'reflective diary' or 'log-book'. This enabled me to ensure that the steps I was taking in my research were systematic and encouraged me to reflect critically upon the actions that I had undertaken. The diagram produced below was designed by myself and my support set (a group of colleagues with whom I shared a commitment to action research).

It sets out in the form of a web the monitoring techniques that can be used in a triangulated research approach. We thought that a spider's web was appropriate as we would only use some strategies for monitoring at any one time and keep others for use at a later date.

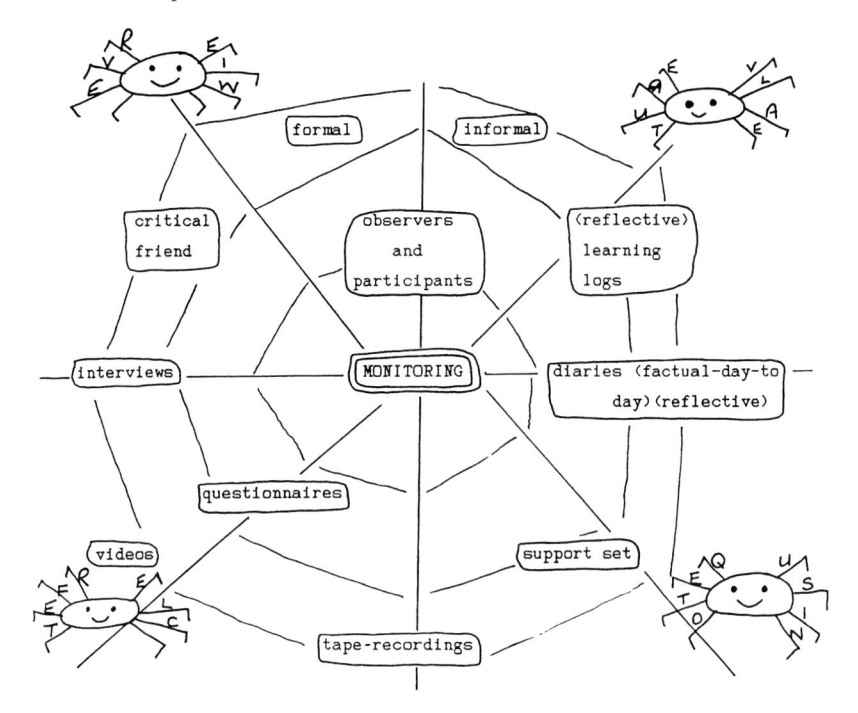

THE CONTEXT OF COLLABORATION

As an outsider brought into the host school to strengthen the management team at a time of considerable pressure for change I was concerned to involve all colleagues in the changes I hoped to initiate. I also had other reasons for involving as many people as possible (colleagues, children, parents) in the assessment process, particularly my belief that the more people involved, then the stronger the assessment process itself in contributing to effective education.

The staff of my host school had previously arranged an in-service training day, but had not begun its detailed planning. I suggested the idea of linking up with my parent school and organising a day on records of achievement based there, the advantage being that the debate could be broadened by wider participation. The staff at both schools agreed to this and planning went ahead with staff from both schools being involved in the setting of the agenda for the day. Subsequent evaluation of the training day through a questionnaire that all participants completed suggested that the day had been enjoyable with high interest levels, assessment had been largely clarified, but that staff were not completely convinced about the feasibility of records of achievement. Comments from my diary elaborate my own reflections on the day:

'I think that the teachers need time to reflect on the implications of this system of records and I will produce a draft document for discussion before the final policy is drawn up..... I think that it is important for the teachers to have some time now to actually start trialling the procedures that they will need to use for implementing records of achievement: (a) good classroom observation techniques; (b) annotating all pieces of work; (c) collecting evidence of attainment; and (d) discussing work with children. All these issues were raised during the training day and the staff have agreed to trial them now. I intend to continue supporting the staff in the classrooms by giving them time to work on their classroom observations and collecting evidence'.

I produced a draft policy document based on the ideas expressed on the training day, and it was discussed at a follow up staff meeting at the host school. Some colleagues continued to express anxiety, particularly about practicalities like storage but it was agreed that I should go ahead and produce the final whole-school policy document on recording achievement (Appendix 1). This was for me a great achievement. I believe that the staff at the host school had gained a sense of identity through their co-operative working. Support had been provided in the tricky problem of assessment and a tool for the promotion of good classroom management skills had been endorsed and accepted by staff members.

RECORDS FOR CHILDREN WITH SPECIAL NEEDS IN MAINSTREAM CLASSES

On my return to my parent school I was determined to continue to use action research to help me develop and trial a new 'record' for children with special educational needs in the mainstream school. In order to develop the record I visited other special schools who shared their ideas and practices with me. Whilst many of their 'records' were interesting, it was clear that they concentrated in many cases on physical rather than academic achievements. This highlighted for me one of the differences between special needs children in a special school and special needs children in a mainstream school. I also spoke to my Local Education Authority advisory teacher for special educational needs who showed me other examples of records.

The trialling was done with a pupil with Downs syndrome (BK) by the class teacher and the classroom assistant who works with BK in the school. This involvement of the classroom assistant was important to me as I felt strongly that all those with important information to contribute about the achievements of children should be included in the process of assessment. I also contacted BK's mother, and explored with her my ideas for recording pupil achievement. She was very enthusiastic and supportive about the new records that I was intending to trial with her daughter. She offered to have one of the records at home so that BK could fill this in immediately she achieved one of her targets - this would have the effect of greatly reinforcing achieved behaviours and then BK could bring the record into school so that her school colleagues, both peer and teacher, could congratulate and reinforce her achievements.

My belief in the need for several different people to be involved in implementing a successful record of achievement had initially been based on ad hoc professional observation but as I had gathered more people into the network of recording achievement and reflected on their contributions these ideas became more structured. I was finally confirmed in my views about the value of considering the contributions of people from different sources in recording the achievement of children by comparing two different sets of records. The first belonged to a child who had special educational needs but until the present had received little extra classroom or parental support (RA), and the second belonged to the child who had been at the centre of the trialling of the new record (BK). The primary difference between the records of RA and BK lay in the way a variety of interested personages had been encouraged to contribute to BK's records - parents, teachers, classroom assistants, teacher for the hearing impaired and BK, the child herself. RA, on the other hand, had assessment records that had been constructed in the traditional teacher oriented way, and which were mainly concerned with progress in curriculum areas. In terms of an all-round picture, BK has the most complete record with achievements at home being given equal weight with achievements at school - a re-dressing of the equation of education equalling schooling. The differences between the two documents also points up the way that some children, especially those with special educational needs, may not be making enormous strides in terms of the National Curriculum, but may be achieving well in other areas - areas of considerable significance - and which should equally well be recorded and applauded.

The best records are those which have involved the child in the target-setting process and the recording of achievement. Children have much useful and important information about how they feel about a task and what they have had to do to achieve it. For assessment to be truly effective, therefore, it is important that the child develops a sense of ownership of the records of achievement document and is proud of his/her achievements. BK as a case in point has shown considerable pride in her achievements and still often stops me in the corridor to demonstrate or tell me about them. For example, in May 1991 BK targeted skipping as one of the things she would like to be able to do. June 1991 saw the enthusiastic recording of eighteen skips—a true personal recording of achievement. (See figs 2 & 3).

The role of the pupil in his/her own assessment is crucial and, although consultation between teacher and child is important, the system of assessment should allow the pupils the opportunity to contribute elements which are entirely their own. Parents too have a very important role to play in the formulation of the record. One of my main priorities at the beginning of the project was to involve BK's parents as soon and as fully as possible. Their interest allowed BK's achievements such as 'wash dishes'; 'make my bed'; and so on, to be recorded adequately. Even for children without the degree of special educational need exhibited by BK the input from the home environment provides the flesh on the bones of school performance. Of

76 *Developing Primary Schools through Action Research*

	I WOULD LIKE TO BE ABLE TO...	
Date		Achieved Signed / Date
first May	6 Skips	✓ 13th May
13 May	swim 8 widths	missed a lot of swimming because of ear trouble.

Fig 2

	I AM ABLE TO...	
		Month & Year
☺ 8.5.91	Wash Dishes	(with help)
☺ 8.5.91	Make my bed	
☺	tens and units adds take away	13.5.91
☺	print graphs on the computer	
☺	18 skips	

Fig 3

course, many special educational needs children do not have the many sources of support afforded to BK, and a consequence of this is that the child's records will not be so detailed and informative. RA's records relied solely on the classroom teacher working with the child and these lack the fully-rounded quality evidenced by those of BK.

REFLECTIONS

And what are the implications of this for my own practice? My experiences as a seconded teacher to a special school, combined with a belief that we were not fully supporting those children with special educational needs in the mainstream school when it came to assessment, had led me to look at the ways in which all interested parties could be involved productively in the assessment process. The participation of parents seems to me to be crucial, and I have found that the majority of parents are sufficiently interested in their child's education to welcome the opportunity to have an input into the record. We in this first school have just started looking into the possibility of negotiating some kind of contract with parents which will actually ask them to commit themselves to participating in the records of achievement scheme.

My research has confirmed for me the view that qualitative assessment, as evidenced in parts of a record of achievement document, should be given as much weight as the more quantitative aspects evidenced by Standardised Assessment Tests. A case study of BK's progress and activities and her delight in her targeted achievements provided contributive evidence for this view. By making sure that the reasons for including items of 'achievement' in the record are clear, the record becomes both formative and diagnostic, two key elements for effective assessment. I believe that a good record of achievement will be ongoing and show continuity and progression in the child's all-round development. The records should contain several examples from each curriculum area and include also achievements at home or in clubs. This ensures that a picture of the 'whole child' will emerge and not be limited to a simple accumulation of academic achievements. This is good practice for all children, not just those with special educational needs; although it is clear that special educational needs children can benefit particularly from this approach.

There is no doubt that implementing a good system of Records of Achievement with their emphasis on both qualitative and quantitative assessment, places great demand on time from teachers who are already overwhelmed by the increased workload imposed by the implementation of the National Curriculum. Once entered into, the problems associated with instigating an effective record of achievement policy seem formidable. Cost, storage, time and commitment become crucial obstacles. However, my own particular research gives indications that the outcomes of such a policy ultimately outweigh the initial difficulties and, once the initial setting-up of the system has been completed, it will actually relieve some of the burden that reliance on a less child centred method of assessment imposes.

APPENDIX ONE

The School Record of Achievement is
(1) A collection of information designed to give a broad picture of the child's growing academic, social and physical achievement both in and out of school.
(2) A means of identifying strengths, weaknesses and progress.
(3) a positive means of sharing information between child, teacher, parent and future establishment (institution or workplace).

Its Aims Are
(1) To motivate the child by involving him/her in goal setting and encouraging a positive self image.
(2) To establish effective partnerships between teacher/parent/child.
(3) To collect readily accessible evidence of the child's growing academic, social and physical achievement.
(4) To build a formative record of achievement and attainment, integral to the learning process.
(5) To facilitate continuity and the efficient transfer of information.

Its Content
(1) Is in three elements
    - a personal biography
    - a portfolio of selected annotated work
    - an attainment record

Its Ownership Is Corporate
To overcome any misunderstanding that to 'own' is to 'possess' the strands will be:
(1) the school during the child's stay
(2) the education system at transfer
(3) the child **finally**

Accessibility Is
(1) immediate - to all teaching staff
(2) by request - to the child
(3) by appointment - to parents
(4) never - to any unauthorised person

The Elements Are
(A) **The Biography:- including**
    (a) personal details
    (b) **necessary** medical information
    (c) a pre-school/process record
    (d) a record of other achievements e.g. music, sport, social
    (e) a record of interests
(a) and (b) will be held centrally. Other items will be class based and updated periodically.

(B) **The Portfolio**

    Content:- from a large termly collection of agreed inclusions to an end of year manageable selection.

    Timescale:- collected week by week. Reviewed termly, sifted and agreed annually.

Selective Criteria

    (a) A partnership approach (teacher/child)
    (b) Representative of overall achievements
    (c) Showing new and breakthrough achievements
    (d) Representative of a variety of curriculum/ cross curriculum areas
    (e) Representative of the current topic

(C) **The Record of Attainment**

    To be discussed.

Practicalities

(1) Each child to have classroom file prior to selection
(2) Each child to have A4 folder for final selection and transfer
(3) Large or 3D items to be considered seperately e.g. photographs
(4) Each classroom to have a suitable storage facility with locks

Use Of Exercise Books

These equally belong to the child with some teacher control, e.g. a book used for rough work or odd jobs is not necessarily seen by parents in education terms. Pages can be photocopied (or removed) for inclusion in folio. Must be marked regularly and dated. Comments should always be positive and informative and should not negate confidence. Unused pages should be carefully removed before sending home.

Resource Implications

(1) Filing/storage
(2) AVA - cameras, video, photocopying, etc.
(3) Space
(4) Time

10. Formulating a School Policy on Assessment for 3-8 Year Old Children

Brenda Spencer

This action research was set within a first school of 265 children and 11 teaching staff inclusive of myself as head teacher. When I took up the post of head teacher in January 1990, the school, in common with all primary schools, was facing the need to agree and implement policy in response to the swift and all embracing changes wrought by the Education Reform Act 1988. These curricular changes encompassed the full breadth of the curriculum - arts, sciences, humanities, mathematics and physical education. However the most radical change was the requirement to assess the achievement of seven year old children formally.

Summer 1991 saw the introduction of formal testing in the form of Standard Assessment Tasks in the core subjects English, mathematics and science for seven year old children. The development of a wide reaching policy on assessment for the whole school was necessary to put these 'tasks' into a meaningful context incorporating a wider view of assessment. The research project was designed to involve staff in formulating a whole school policy on assessment from 3-8 years that included the idea of ongoing evaluation of classroom practice as well as the intention to use assessment to aid planning, inform teaching strategies and indicate what children could do.

THE IMPORTANCE OF VALUES

It was important to me that the policy developed would be underpinned by certain values. These concerned ideas relating to assessment and also the nature of staff involvement in developing work within the school. I believed that:

(a) methods of assessment should arise from whole school consideration;
(b) assessment should be integral to the educational process that children experience;
(c) assessment should be practical and realistic to administer;
(d) assessment should recognise the positive achievement of children;
(e) assessment should aid teachers to plan the way forward in providing an appropriate education for the children;
(f) assessment should help the diagnosis of children's difficulties;
(g) assessment should be a tool for evaluation of the effectiveness of the educational provision of the school.

I believed that these values should underpin all my actions and be the focus for the direction of my planned improvement in both my own practice and school assessment practice.

THE IMPORTANCE OF COLLABORATION

In tackling assessment we needed to establish what we understood good practice to be and to decide how we would set about it. Whole staff inservice education and training and discussion (including all teachers and nursery nurses) was a possible means of establishing our aims and objectives and devising strategies to achieve them. I believed that the quality of our policy formulation would depend on how informed staff were about good practice in assessment and the national requirements. I saw my role as enabling staff to be fully informed about good assessment procedures and the government/ L.E.A. requirements for assessment, in order that a wise and workable policy could be formulated and tailored to the local needs and philosophy of our school. Because we were forced to second-guess changes in curricula structure (mathematics and science particularly) and to recognise that the assessment arrangements for year 1990/91 were not going to be repeated in 1991/92, we placed emphasis on agreeing the principles, the aims and the ethos in which to conduct our assessment work. The research study was about the beginning of a process - in terms of planning, implementing and evaluating an assessment policy that we were only at the planning and beginning-to-implement stage.

METHOD OF WORKING

This was an enquiry which addressed real issues related to the classroom and the curriculum. The insider's perspective was regarded as a rich resource in deciding relevant areas of enquiry and in providing appropriate interpretations, actions and outcomes. It was an enquiry which was concerned with teachers becoming innovators within the field of assessment. The method of research which could support such a personal enquiry was action research.

Action research is not a detached enquiry. Gurney (1989, p.25) states 'action research begins with a concept of what we are trying to do'. In contrast to other forms of research the direction of the change is not dictated by an external researcher. The marriage of the two roles of competent technician and thoughtful reflective educator is achieved through this mode of enquiry. This results in enquiries being conducted which address practical issues that concern value and quality and explore relationships. Action research also encourages what McNiff has called a ' generative capacity to allow for spontaneous creative episodes'. She says:

> 'Action research should offer the capacity to deal with a number of problems at the same time by allowing the spirals to develop spin-off spirals.... Generative action research enables a teacher-researcher to address many different problems at one time without losing sight of the main issue' (McNiff, 1988/1992 p.43).

The methods of fact finding, data gathering and evaluation that I used in my research have depended largely on descriptive accounts by individuals working in a small school. The data gathering for the purpose of monitoring took several forms: staff responses to an initial questionnaire about their assessment practices; minutes and taped recordings of meetings; recorded discussions with a critical friend; draft and final documentation about policy; and a reflective diary. Where possible I used the method of triangulation: getting a picture of the same event from several different sources of evidence.

The personal reflective diary and the opportunity to discuss issues with my critical friend were key factors in my evaluation of the work. The diary contained the plans, agenda and record of staff's contributions. The evolution of my ideas of how the project should progress is delineated. Finally my own personal reflections on the conduct of each meeting gives an additional perspective on the situation. The rigour and discipline of this way of working is supported by Richard Winter who argues:

> 'the practical necessity for practitioner researchers to work in such a way that they preserve their own professional role constitutes a rigorous intellectual discipline, ensuring that the conclusions of the work were broadly based, balanced, and comprehensively grounded in the perceptions of a variety of others' (Winter, 1989, p.23).

My critical fiend was a member of staff chosen for her quality of critical honesty. In addition she was class teacher of children undergoing Standardised Assessment Tests. Her role was to comment on the development of the project and evaluate my role. Kemmis and McTaggart support this way of working. They argue that:

> 'A distinguishing factor of action research is that those affected by planned changes have primary responsibility for deciding on courses of action which seem likely to lead to an improvement, and for evaluating the results of strategies tried out in practice' (Kemmis and McTaggart, 1982, p.6).

I believe that my critical friend, a key member of staff, was able to take on this responsibility and to some extent mitigate the criticism that the project was more a management tool than a grass roots practice of managing change (Griffiths, 1990, p.43). And this despite the fact that it was a government initiative that forced assessment on first schools. My critical friend helped me evaluate how far I enabled staff to become informed and develop their own policy of assessment.

Figure 1. Chronological Diary of Events

Date	Activity	Research
1990 October	Discussions with Year 2 teachers and assessment Moderators.	Group/individual meetings.
	Clarify government requirements for assessment. Clarifying Local Education Authority needs.	Local Education Authority/Department of Education and Science circular. Non statutory guidelines. Newspapers. National Curriculum Council & School Examination & Assessment Council documents.
November	Investigating current assessment practice in school.	Questionnaire to staff; inservice education and training day.
	Planning inservice work with Local Education Authority Moderator, advisers & year 2 teachers.	Group/individual meetings.
December	Agree timetable for teacher assessment.	Group meetings.
	Agree principles for teacher assessment.	Group meetings.
January 1991	Start planning for new policy.	Inservice education and training day.
	Involve all staff in drafting policy on assessment.	Staff meetings.
	Agree procedures for moderation.	Staff meeting.
	Standard setting.	Group meetings.
February	Involve staff in drafting policy on records of Achievement.	Staff meeting.
	Discussion of portfolios.	Group meetings.
March	Redraft portfolio document.	Staff meetings.
March/April	Implement/analyze Standardised Assessment Tests.	Group meetings.

CHRONOLOGICAL DIARY OF EVENTS

The diary entries (figure 1) document the chronological progress of the research. Certain events were particularly important in establishing points for reflective reference. I think that three of these are of particular interest: (a) the questionnaire analysis of existing practice; (b) my attempt to ascertain if I was involving the staff in the research; (c) the rationale for the portfolio policy.

QUESTIONNAIRE ANALYSIS OF CURRENT PRACTICE

The early part of the project (October) was concerned with reconnaissance: clarifying government directives about National Curriculum Key Stage 1 Assessment and discussing their implications with year 2 teachers and Moderators. It was becoming clear that we needed to clarify a picture of the current assessment practice in different classrooms in the school. Information relating to individual teachers' assessment practices was collected from a questionnaire they completed in November. Seven teachers were asked to provide information about their current practices in the following areas:

(a) formal modes of assessment

(b) informal modes of assessment

(c) rationale behind informal assessments

(d) use of children's work as evidence in assessment

(e) use of classroom observation techniques

(f) the partnership of planning assessment

This information was instrumental in designing the form and content of the inservice education and training that would precede the formulation of a whole school policy on assessment.

Analysis of questionnaire returns
Formal assessment

The systems in harness at School were MEND, Bury Infant Checklist, National Foundation for Educational Research Reading Test and Non Verbal Reasoning Test. The reading and non verbal reasoning tests were used by the Local Education Authority to allocate Language Support Services to children in need. They were summative, not diagnostic tests. Those children with a wide discrepancy between performances and intelligence were selected for support. Bury Infant Checklist was a diagnostic test applied to children a term after their entrance into reception. Children's language, numerical, application and learning strategies were assessed. MEND was a Local Authority record for teachers to analyze and record children's special needs. On reflecting upon this information it seemed that the purposes served by the formal assessment carried out in school were incomplete in that future planning and evaluating the school's provisions were not currently being addressed by our formal tests.

Informal assessment

The informal assessment carried out by staff served in the main, formative purposes. This planning moved in two directions:
- planning work to match ability
- planning the composition of children's groups

None of the staff mentioned using assessment for planning future curriculum content. This could arise from record keeping procedures. One member of staff used informal strategies above and beyond Bury Infant Checklist, MEND and reading tests, that is, formal tests for diagnosis of areas of specific difficulty. Another used informal methods for 'getting to know the whole child'.

It seemed to me that a balanced picture of a child could begin to emerge by combining the formal and informal modes of assessment used. But the picture was still incomplete. A summative assessment of a child was only being obtained by an outdated reading test administered at 7. No other aspect of the child's performance was assessed from a summative point of view. Neither informal nor formal testing was being used to analyze the adequacy of the school's provision or for looking at our developmental needs.

Gaps identified in assessment practice

The Task Group on Assessment and Testing exhorts teachers 'to exploit a wide range of modes of presentation, operation and response, and then numerous combinations, in order to widen the range of pupil's abilities that they reflect and so to enhance their educational validity' (Department of Education and Science, 1988a).

The formal tests used by the school were presented either as written or pictorial test papers. The tasks children engaged in for the purposes of formal tests allowed for a mental mode alone. The responses dictated by the formal tests were written or pictorial with the greater emphasis on the written mode.

The informal practice of assessment used by the staff did not often include presentation of assessment tasks but rather involved observation of children going about their daily class work. Teachers made mention of observing children's strategies for reading, writing, applying mathematical concepts and operating in a social context. Such activities involved the full range of operation modes: mental, written, practical and oral. However, this seemed to be by chance rather than as a result of a coherent policy for teacher assessment. The full range of response modes do not seem to be explored by our informal test, either. However, examples of work were collected from children as evidence of achievement for diagnostic purposes and to evaluate and show progression. A much richer picture of the child was being obtained by a combination of formal tests, informal observations and analysis of portfolios of work.

If teacher assessment was to make a significant contribution, then certain issues had to be addressed by our policy. One teacher described her guilt at taking time to stand back and observe. This activity needed to be given status; organisation and use of teacher's time needed to be modified. It was an issue that needed to be addressed by all the staff. T'.e majority of observation was done incidentally, without any structure. In summary, it seemed that:

- Teacher observation needed a higher profile
- Observations needed to be structured
- Children must be allowed to respond to tests in a variety of planned ways
- The full range of purposes of assessment needed to be exploited
- Assessment needed to be applied to a wider spectrum of the curriculum
- Portfolios of work needed to be collected purposefully

The questionnaire returns containing teachers' accounts of their current practice of assessment provided a rich source of information upon which to base the content of subsequent inservice education and training. The inservice education and training day in January 1991 was able to draw upon the results of the questionnaire to focus teachers in their task of deciding about a policy for assessment. At that inservice education and training day the first compilation of decisions was made by the staff of the kinds of work to be collected and assessed with the reasons for those choices.

INVOLVING THE WHOLE STAFF

An important issue in my investigation was my aim to enable all the staff to contribute to the formulation of our policy on assessment. I was concerned that members of staff would pay lip service to proposed changes out of deference to my head teacher status rather than out of real commitment on their part. I was also unsure about the extent to which I enabled staff to contribute to decision-making in a staff meeting. One small side spiral of my research was to do with investigating my practice in a staff meeting. I asked two teachers to observe me chairing a discussion over a ten minutes period. They used Flanders Interactive Analysis to identify different types of excluding and including behaviour. The monitoring staff, who were asked to conduct their observation at a time of their choice, both chose the same period - the beginning of the meeting. Whilst this produces a possibility of comparison of perception, thereby giving an element of objectivity, different parts of a meeting elicit certain behaviour. Beginnings are dominated by introductions and explanations, ends by summarising techniques. Bearing in mind that staff carrying out the survey were commenting on the head teacher's behaviour (and could have been inhibited from reporting honestly) none of the excluding types of behaviour were reported during the time of observation, that is, dominating, manipulating, blocking, belittling, distracting, splitting hairs, excluding. Dominant forms of behaviour (those which occurred three times or more in the ten minute period) were initiating, clarifying, seeking information, mediating, giving information and expressing group feelings. Other forms of behaviour occurring less often were integrating, encouraging/supporting, compromising, consensus testing, and being open. This analysis was supported by an overall verbal summary of the meeting by the two teachers.

My personal reflections on the meeting agreed in substance with the findings of the Interaction Analysis. Clarification and summarising were dominant modes of behaviour. This was carried out to ensure that the staff's views were being translated accurately in the draft form of the policy. Areas where I felt my handling of meetings could improve related to compilation of the agenda. If this had been drawn up in greater detail, possibly staff may have been able to orientate their minds on the issues more quickly. I also had a tape recording of the meeting which (on analysis) confirmed that some members of the group contributed valuably while others were more reticent. This suggested the need for me to integrate colleagues more effectively. Whilst the observers did not accuse me of dominating the discussions I felt that the tapes did suggest I need to listen for a greater period of the time. Many of my contributions were related to keeping the discussions on task and within the framework of the agenda, or in clarifying government requirements.

The result of the observation gave me direction for improving the leadership of subsequent discussions. Integrating, encouraging and supporting members of the group should have had a higher profile if I were really intent on incorporating the whole staff in the act of policy formulation. One of the year two teachers did not contribute at all. The observer drew my attention to the fact that some colleagues were seated outside my immediate field of vision. This was not helpful in drawing out their opinions. It is quite clear that provision of a forum for members of staff to formulate their policy on assessment is not sufficient. More details need to be given before meetings to allow people to orientate their thoughts. Reticent members of staff need to be drawn into discussions. Simple monitoring of seating plans will be helpful in achieving wider contribution to discussions.

EVALUATING THE DRAFT PORTFOLIO POLICY

A major aspect of the whole school assessment policy that was emerging was to do with the production of a policy on portfolios. This aspect of the policy attempts to address our requirement for teacher assessment by evaluating children's work. Items of work and observations on children's activities are collected at agreed points during the year. This together with Standardised Assessment Tests provides the complete picture of a child's development as envisaged by the Task Group on Assessment and Testing.

We thought that it was important to be clear about the purposes underpinning the collation of the portfolios. Formative, diagnostic and summative aspects of assessment are addressed by systematic collection of children's work. By collecting specific items of work or observing children applying certain skills and knowledge at designated times during the year, the progress the child has made from the year before should be evident. This was one of the considerations the Task Group on Assessment and Testing found to be of importance in good assessment.

The portfolio is designed to indicate the child's general level of performance, primarily to facilitate transition between classes, schools and teachers. The summative aspect of assessment arises here. However it should reflect the achievements over a wide field of experience. To this end the portfolio incorporates evidence from a broad curricular spectrum. The school policy acknowledges the importance of parents appreciating the extent of their children's learning. This significance to the staff of this factor was evident in their discussions which I recorded. For example: SD: 'It's always important for parents to understand why we're doing this'. The summative aspect is also addressed in the child's best interests. It is inevitable that some children will not perform to ability during a formal testing situation. We regard it as important to collect evidence for moderating purposes in case a child's performance in a Standardised Assessment Test does not reflect true ability. The significance to teachers of using careful evaluation of children's work for diagnostic purposes is clear from the following comments I recorded during staff meetings: BS: 'What you are talking about there is a tool for diagnosis'; and SR: 'Perhaps some sort of miscue which reflects reading strategies, reading behaviour rather than number of books read. See the actual process. What sort of Mathematics they're using'. These remarks were translated in the policy to written affirmation of the need to furnish material to act as a diagnostic tool.

The questionnaire revealed that neither the formal nor informal modes of assessment previously used in school furnished evidence of effectiveness of the school provision. Our policy does not appear to address this issue either. The government envisaged that Standardised Assessment Tests would provide an indicator of good and bad schools and would highlight areas of weakness. My personal concern is that a simple record of the levels achieved by the children in a particular school, if not supplemented with information about their abilities, tells us little about the 'added value' provided by schools. We therefore are unable to evaluate their effectiveness fairly. The absence of an evaluative tool in our assessment procedures will need to be tackled at a future date.

The policy meets the concerns of the staff to give the children opportunity to express the full range of their abilities: for example,

BS: 'A piece of writing is not going to cover all our needs and what we're looking at.'

DC: 'We don't want to emphasise writing in Science. We want to emphasise the practical, the actual doing it.'

CH: 'To show the roundness of their education.'

LD: 'We need tapes of children who are articulate but don't write very well. They don't really get credit.'

DC: 'If you see a piece of work which has applied Mathematics to a problem. I think that's the sort of thing.'

SR: 'See the actual process. What sort of Mathematics they're using. Initiatives have forced assessment on first schools. My critical friend helped me evaluate how far I enabled the staff to become informed and develop their own policy of assessment.'

The questionnaire intimated that whilst the formal modes of presentation, operation and response to assessment currently employed by our formal testing were narrow, this was not the case for informal assessments. However, these assessments were incidental and unstructured and therefore could not guarantee giving the children a real opportunity to reflect their abilities and needs. Furthermore, because these assessments were idiosyncratic to each class the important requirement of providing a picture of a child's progress was not facilitated.

The Standardised Assessment Tests did allow for a variety of modes with differing success. In particular, the construction of a game for the Mathematical assessment allowed children to explore the problem in any way their imaginations fancied. Unfortunately it did little to assess their application of mathematical concepts for which it was designed. It is important that our practices will be varied and 'task-orientated'.

The presentation mode of the assessment will inevitably be varied. The portfolio comprises either examples of work or observation schedules of children applying their skills and knowledge to practical tasks. The method of delivery of the tasks within the normal classroom context will be varied. Of the examples given by the Task Group on Assessment and Testing the delivery through the computer is the area most likely to be neglected. This may be something we will need to examine.

The collections of work and areas of observation reflect the broad and balanced curriculum. The children will have ample opportunity to work in mental, written, practical and oral modes and the final responses to the tasks will also be wide-ranging. The observation schedules in particular will focus on the children's scientific and mathematical problem solving abilities.

The real weakness of our practice highlighted in the questionnaires was the haphazard nature of our assessment. The policy addresses that issue in several ways.

- timing of assessment of different areas of the curriculum is now set out clearly and spread through the year to avoid difficulties of manageability;
- criteria by which pieces of work should be assessed are clearly thought through and articulated;
- teachers make a claim to exercise their professional judgement, not in a haphazard way but within their understanding of good practice underpinned by a sound theoretical basis;
- teacher assessment is carried out across the age range, not merely at year 2, thereby developing the skills of the whole staff and allowing a comprehensive picture of a child's needs and abilities to emerge.

WHAT WAS ACHIEVED

The following claims may be substantiated by the research:
- The staff have responded effectively in applying their expertise to the need for thoughtful teacher assessment in an intelligent, task-orientated policy for assessment;
- The use of action research has operated at 'grass roots level practice, not appearing merely as a 'management tool'. The teachers had responsibility for the changes they proposed in response to legislative demands for assessment.

IMPLICATIONS

Future cycles of action will necessarily include:
- examining ways of applying evaluative assessment to the school. This may be through devising performance indicators;
- exploring the strategies proposed for drawing reticent members of staff into discussions;
- analysis at the end of the academic year of the collections of work and observation schedules. Are they serving our desired aims for teacher assessment?
- analysis of the combined picture provided by Standardised Assessment Tests and teacher assessment to see if the full picture of a child is obtained.

BIBLIOGRAPHY

Ainscow M. (1988) 'Beyond the eyes of the monster: an analysis of recent trends in assessment and recording' *Support for Learning* 3 (3) pp. 149-53.

AMA et al (1991) *Assessment Under the National Curriculum Joint Union Advice on Workload* College Press Ltd.

BERA Task Group (1991) 'Different ways of killing the cat or using the SAT'. *Education* 18th October 1991.

Bolton E. (1985) 'Assessment techniques and approaches: an overview' in Department of Education and Science (1985) *Better Schools*, London: HMSO.

Black H. (1989) *Aspects of Assessment: A Primary Perspective.* SARSU (?).

Black P. J. (1987) *Task group on Assessment and Testing.* Department of Education and Science.

Broadfoot, P (1988) The National Assessment Framework and records of Achievement. in H. Torrance (ed.). *National Assessment and Testing: A Research Response.* Kendal: BERA.

Cable J (1990) *National Curriculum Assessment Arrangements.* (Letter to head teachers), L B Merton.

Carr, W. (1989) *Quality in teaching.* London: The Falmer Press.

Dean J (1983) *Organizing Learning in Primary Schools.* London: Croom Helm.

Department of Education and Science (1987) *National Curriculum 5-16. A Consultation Document.* London: HMSO.

Department of Education and Science (1988a) *National Curriculum: Task Group on Assessment and Testing: A Report.* London: HMSO.

Department of Education and Science and the Welsh Office (1988b) *National Curriculum: Task Group on Assessment and Testing Report: A Digest for Schools.* London: HMSO.

Department of Education and Science (1988c) *National Curriculum : From Policy to Practice.* London: HMSO.

Department of Education and Science (1989a) *Records of Achievement National Steering Committee: Report.* London: HMSO.

Department of Education and Science (1989b) *Educational Reform Act 1988: School Curriculum and Assessment.* Circular 5/89, Department of Education and Science.

Department of Education and Science (1990a). *The Education (National Curriculum) (Assessment Arrangements for English, Mathematics and Science) Order 1990.* London: HMSO.

Department of Education and Science (1990b). *Education Reform Act 1988: The Education (National Curriculum) (Assessment Arrangements for English, Mathematics and Science) Order 1990.* Circular 9/90. London: HMSO.

Department of Education and Science (1990c) *Speeches on Education: National Curriculum and Assessment.* HMSO.

Department of Education and Science (1990) Circular 8/90.

Duncan (P) and Dunn (D) (1985) *Why Primary Teachers Should Know About Assessment.* London: Hodder and Stoughton.

Follows, M. (1992) *How can I establish a cooperative and collaborative community of teachers whilst implementing national curriculum key stage one assessment?* Unpublished dissertation. London: Kingston Polytechnic.

Gulbenkian Foundation (1982) *The Arts in School.* London: Oyez Press.

Gurney, M. (1989) 'Implementor or innovator? A teacher's challenge to the restrictive paradigm of traditional research', in P Lomax (ed.). *The Management of Change.* Clevedon: Multi Lingual Matters.

Griffiths, M. (1990) 'Action research: grassroot practice or management tool?' in P Lomax (ed.). *Managing Staff Development in Schools: an Action Research Approach.* Clevedon: Multi Lingual Matters.

Her Majesty's Inspectorate. (1989) *The effectiveness of small special schools.*

Hopkins, D. (1991) 'Ever smaller and more manageable.' *Times Educational Supplement. September 27.*

Inner London Education Authority.(1985) *Improving Primary Schools.* London: Inner London Education Authority.

Kemmis, S. and McTaggart, R. (1982) *The action research planner.* Australia: Deakin University.

Lomax, P. (1986) 'Action researchers' action research: A symposium. *British Journal of In-Service Education, 13 (1).*

Lomax, P. (1989) *The Management of Change (BERA Dialogues 1).* Clevedon: Multi Lingual Matters.

Lomax, P. (1990a) *Managing Staff Development in Schools (BERA Dialogues 3).* Clevedon: Multi Lingual Matters.

Lomax, P. (1990b) An action research approach to developing staff in schools, in P Lomax (ed.).. *Managing Staff Development in Schools (BERA Dialogues 3.)* Clevedon: Multi Lingual Matters.

Lomax, P. (1991a). *Managing Better Schools and Colleges* (BERA Dialogues 5). Clevedon: Multi Lingual Matters.

Lomax, P. (1991b). 'Peer review and action research', in P. Lomax (ed.) *Managing Better Schools and Colleges (BERA Dialogues 5).* Clevedon: Multi Lingual Matters.

Lomax, P. (1992, April). *Managing Change and the Empowerment of Schools.* Paper presented at the Fourth Research Conference of the British Educational Management and Administration Society. Nottingham.

London Borough of Croydon (1986) *Guidelines on Assessment.* Croydon: London Borough of Croydon.

London Borough of Croydon. (1991) *Managing Teacher Assessment.* Croydon: London Borough of Croydon.

London Borough of Merton (1991) *The Curriculum from 3-19: a statement of policy.* Merton: London Borough of Merton.

London Borough of Hillingdon (1985) *Guidelines on Assessment* Hillingdon Assessment Support Team, Hillingdon.

McBride, R. (1989) *The in-service training of teachers.* London: The Falmer Press.

McNiff, J. (1988) *Action Research: Principles and Practice.* London: Macmillan/ Routledge, London & New York, (1992).

NAHT (1990) *National Curriculum Helpline Guidance Note 11: National Curriculum Assessment.* National Association of Head Teachers.

Plowden Report (1967) *Children and their Primary Schools.* London: HMSO.

Satterley, D. (1989). *Assessment in Schools.* London: Blackwell.

School Examination and Assessment Council (1989) *Records of Achievement in Primary Schools.* London: HMSO.

School Examination and Assessment Council (1990) *A Guide to Teacher Assessment : Pack A. Teacher Assessment in the Classroom.* London: Heinemann.

School Examination and Assessment Council (1990) *A Guide to Teacher Assessment : Pack B. Teacher Assessment in the School.* London: Heinemann.

School Examination and Assessment Council (1990) *A Guide to Teacher Assessment : Pack C. A Source Book for Teacher Assessment.* London: Heinemann.

School Examination and Assessment Council (1990) *SEAC Recorder No 6.* HMSO.

School Examination and Assessment Council (1991) *National Curriculum Assessment : A moderator's handbook.* London: HMSO.

School Examination and Assessment Council (1991) *National Curriculum Assessment ; Responsibilities of LEAs.* London: HMSO.

Surrey Local Education Authority (1988) *Towards an Assessment Policy for the Primary School.* Surrey: Local Education Authority.

Thomas N. (1990) *Primary Education from Plowden to 1990s* Lewis: Falmer Press.

Torrance, H. (1988) *National Assessment and Testing : A Research Response.* Kendal: BERA.

Whitehead, J. and Foster, D. (1984) 'Action research and professional educational development'. in *Classroom Action Research Network Bulletin No. 6 pp. 41-45.*

Winter, R. (1989) *Learning from Experience.* London: Falmer Press.